the SUPER DAD MYTH

the SUPER DAD MYTH

*Doing Just Enough: A Low-Bar Guide
to Raising Kids Who Won't Totally Hate You*

J. ROBB CRUSER

BOOKLOGIX®
Alpharetta, GA

Although the author and publisher have made every effort to ensure that the information in this book was correct at the time of first publication, the author and publisher do not assume and hereby disclaim any liability to any party for any loss, damage, or disruption caused by errors or omissions, whether such errors or omissions result from negligence, accident, or any other cause.

Copyright © 2025 J. Robb Cruser

All rights reserved. No part of this book may be reproduced or transmitted in any form or by any means, electronic or mechanical, including photocopying, recording, or any information storage and retrieval system, without permission in writing from the author.

ISBN: 978-1-63183-347-2 – Paperback
ISBN: 978-1-63183-840-8 – ePub

These ISBNs are the property of BookLogix for the express purpose of sales and distribution of this title. The content of this book is the property of the copyright holder only. BookLogix does not hold any ownership of the content of this book and is not liable in any way for the materials contained within. The views and opinions expressed in this book are the property of the Author/Copyright holder, and do not necessarily reflect those of BookLogix.

Library of Congress Control Number: 2021909979

⊚This paper meets the requirements of ANSI/NISO Z39.48-1992 (Permanence of Paper)

Scripture taken from the Holy Bible, New International Version®. Copyright © 1973, 1978, 1984 by International Bible Society. Used by permission of Zondervan Publishing House. All rights reserved.

Cover image by Davide D'Amico
Cover design by Virtually Possible Designs
Illustrations by Soyelchico

I dedicate this book to "No One," because that is who clamors for it.

No one ever accuses me of being a parenting guru. No one asks for my parenting advice. No one invites me to speak on parenting topics. No one asked that I write this book. And why should they?

Let's be honest. How many fathers really want others to tell them how to raise their own children? Not many. And among those, how many would pay someone for it? Even fewer. And of that tiny group, how many would spend money on a nonexpert's opinions and stories? It's incredibly presumptuous for someone to think their advice is valuable about a child and parent they've never met. It's sheer arrogance. I'm at the front of that outrage line.

Is this where I dedicate the book to my own five children? Absolutely not! My hypocrisy goes only so far. This book is a selfish vanity project, sparked by my objection to youth tattoos—more on that later. For years, this book has been an irritating yoke, I'm relieved to finally throw off in the irrelevant abyss. The irony? In writing this so-called parenting book, I've sacrificed countless hours that could have been spent nurturing my relationship with my own children. How head-shakingly sad. (Although, perhaps they appreciated the break from me.) On the other hand, is it really a parenting book or something else entirely?

In summary, I dedicate this unsolicited, nonexpert book to its expected audience: No one.

CONTENTS

Opening Challenge … ix
Introduction … xi

Part I
Follow Me: The Disappearing Dad under the Sun … 1

   Chapter 1: The Childhood Deadly Decisions … 3
   Chapter 2: The Childhood Damaging Decisions … 41
   Chapter 3: The Childhood Dumb Decisions … 81
   Chapter 4: The Reconciling Dad: Horizontal Reconciliation (Child-to-Parent) … 87
   Chapter 5: The Reconciling Dad: Vertical Reconciliation (Child-to-God) … 161

Part II
Follow Him: The Forever Father above the Sun … 173

   Chapter 6: The Cravings Lock … 175
   Chapter 7: The Lies Lock … 185
   Chapter 8: The Doubts Lock … 187
   Chapter 9: The Wager … 193
   Chapter 10: The Gospel Games … 195

Closing and Verdict: Decision Time … 213
Invitation … 215
Acknowledgments … 217

Appendix A: Additional Reading Materials	219
Endnotes	221

OPENING CHALLENGE

THE FIRST QUESTION

Who is your great-grandfather?

. . . Any idea? Or is it a little fuzzy like the picture? Most of us have no clue who our ancestors were after our grandparents. Take this test. Ask your wife, your significant other, your coworker, or a friend the following question: "Who is your great-grandfather?" We predict that nine out of ten times, you will get a completely blank stare. Total crickets. Go ahead. Try it.

So, what truth does this question reveal? Answer: Everyone is forgotten, and sooner than you think.

Unless you are a celebrity, some historical figure, or a rich dude that leaves behind multigenerational wealth, after the grandchildren, our descendants will have no idea who we were or what we did on planet Earth. We'll have zero direct impact on our great-grandchildren. They won't even be able to come up with our names! To them, we're an unknown name on an unknown family tree. So much for leaving a legacy. Fifty years from right now, neither you nor your memory will exist, even to your family—amazing and depressing.

But freeing! Once we accept the limits of self, we can point to a more lasting and satisfying legacy for our children and descendants.

THE FINAL QUESTION

Who is your child's permanent father? The answer will determine *your* destiny. No pressure though.

INTRODUCTION

For some reason, intentional or otherwise, you and I decided to bring a child into this world and continue the human experience. We decided to be *dads*! Good for us. Our lifestyle is the same except for managing some minor interruptions from our little bundles of joy, right?

Wrong.

Our former, childless lives are over, never to return. The biggest adjustment made by every dad is not going from one to two children, nor even three to four children, nor any other combination. No, going from zero to one child is the forever life-changer; it puts us in the dad business.

This is new territory. We start out knowing nothing about being a dad. Since entering adulthood, we've been on the Me Team. We did what we wanted to do, when we wanted to do it. We chose our friends. We chose our activities. We set the schedule. We went to the bathroom when we wanted. We were large and in charge.

That's over now.

We've been traded from the Me Team to a new team: *Team Dad!* We've been signed to an eighteen-year *reverse* contract with a kid option, meaning this contract doesn't pay, *we* do (about $200,000 per kid, depending on the study). And if our kids don't launch into self-sufficient adulthood? They can exercise a contract "option" and stay on the family payroll *indefinitely*. Welcome to the team!

Don't expect any adoration from our culture for being a dad. To the contrary, our culture does not praise much or demand much from dads. When dads walk away from their obligations to their children and their children's mothers, there is no public shaming of the deadbeat dads. The culture quietly yawns. Dads aren't even generous in spirit with each other. Just ask the stay-at-home dads about the cool reactions and sideway glances they receive from the hard-charging career dads. The culture quietly disapproves. Fatherhood is just not as acclaimed as motherhood is. We know it. We live with it. If we doubt that, just ask our government. Mother's Day was declared by Congress and President Woodrow Wilson a national holiday in 1914, over one hundred years ago. And Father's Day? Try fifty-eight years and nine presidents later when, in 1972, Richard Nixon signed into law the observance of Father's Day. And which holiday comes first? You guessed it: Mother's Day.

On the other hand, many in today's culture cast fatherhood as nothing but toil and sacrifice. Oh, and having a large (more than two kids) family? Forget it. Why would anyone take that on? We disagree. For most of us, raising well-adjusted children who contribute to their families and communities will be one of our greatest joys. Childrearing has been described as a "labor of love," which is about right. There is labor involved, to be sure, but love transcends the equation. Why not take up the challenge and awesome responsibility of raising the next generation?

THE SUPER DAD IS A MYTH

Easy, fella. Before taking up the challenge, we need to get real: SUPER DADS DON'T EXIST!

They never did.

Good dads? Yes. Terrific dads? Maybe. But Super Dads? Not so much! There are no Super Dads out there making all the right decisions with the right motives. We need to get over ourselves. The ugly reality is that the average dad spends less than one hour per day accomplishing any meaningful interaction with his children. Most of us are too busy chasing our selfish interests—money, status, possessions, career, power, reputation, comfort, sports teams, hobbies, sex, influence, writing, whatever—to be a Super Dad.

This book does not present an impossible formula to be a Super Dad that none of us can achieve. Besides, even if being a Super Dad were possible, child outcomes are variable. So RELAAAX. We'll never be Super, but we can strive to avoid parental malpractice by being the least bad dad possible.

THE VISION

The purpose of this book is to minimize our acts of parental malpractice, so our children won't hate us and have a better chance of accomplishing *stable and productive lives*, whether in the secular or spiritual realm. And maybe even improve our own lives too.

The purpose of this book is not to raise the next president of the United States. Or a professional athlete. Or a child that changes the world. If you're looking to develop a Super Kid, that is a different hustle and not the subject of this book. Being stable and modestly productive is purpose enough.

If the vision is going to happen, we better know what we're talking about when taking the parental stage—namely, (1) what is our parental *message* to nudge our children in the direction of a stable and productive life, and (2) how can we be effective *messengers* of such a message?

TWO AVAILABLE MESSAGES TO ACCOMPLISH THE VISION

There are only two available parental messages: secular and spiritual. To establish stability, we are going to teach our children the ways of the world or the ways of the eternal, or some combination of both.

TWO AVAILABLE MESSENGERS TO ACCOMPLISH THE VISION

Who are we going to point to as role models for our children to follow? There are only two paternal messengers to speak into our children's lives: the "Disappearing Dad" and the "Forever Father."

Part I invites our children to follow a Disappearing Dad speaking a secular message. Who is the Disappearing Dad? He is *us*—mortal, physical dads who live on Earth under the sun. We are temporary. We start with no paternal experience, but we know enough to demand good *behavior* from our kids to promote a stable and productive life. This is the wide path that most of us model and encourage our children to follow. Like father (earthly), like son.

Part II invites our children to follow someone else: the Forever Father speaking a spiritual message. Who is the Forever Father? He is *Almighty God*—the immortal, spiritual father who lives above the sun. He is eternal. He has infinite paternal experience and encourages total *heart* change from His children (parent and child alike) to promote a stable and productive life, throwing in eternity to boot. This is the narrow path that few model and encourage our children to follow. Like father (almighty), like son.

If the reader is turned off by God or spiritual matters, then stop after Part I. We do not seek to impose a viewpoint that is uninvited. This book makes no demands to change anyone's worldview—political, religious, gender identification, sexual orientation, or otherwise. We don't insist on how you should conduct yourself or raise your children. Besides, there are probably enough people in your life doing that already. We endeavor to leave our ugly self-righteousness at the door and apologize when we fail to do so. Part I is secular, can stand alone to avert parental malpractice, and improve the likelihood of raising a stable child.

It is up to each of us to determine which message and messenger we advance to others, including our children.

THE FOUNDATIONAL ROCK OF RECONCILIATION

Reconciliation is a foundational theme throughout this book. We discuss horizontal reconciliation (man-to-man) and vertical reconciliation (man-to-God) in Chapters 4 and 5, respectively. Regardless of our message, to be effective, we must be *reconciled with our children*, meaning to be in a positive relationship with them. If we are not reconciled with them, we have little voice, little influence, and little chance of nudging them in the direction of a stable and productive live—the purpose of this book. If we are in a broken parent-child relationship, we will not be heard and are shoving them in the wrong direction. Job #1: Be reconciled with our children.

OUR ANGLE: CELEBRITY STORYTELLING

Everybody's got an angle.
So, what's our angle?
Answer: Celebrity stories.
What? That's it?
Yup, that's it. Celebrity stories are the reconciling and teaching mechanism to nudge our children toward a stable life.

In Part I, we'll read interesting, edgy celebrity stories with our children to impart timeless lessons on how to be stable adults. Because we have poor attention spans, each story is less than five minutes. For example, have we read to our teenagers how rapper Tupac Shakur was gunned down on the Vegas strip, his final words being "F★★★ you"? Or how singing icon Whitney Houston drowned in her Beverly Hills hotel bathtub in a drug-induced state? Or how *The Fast and the Furious* movie star Paul Walker was killed when his Porsche Carrera GT was driven into a tree? Ah, yes; all bedtime story classics. Read on, they're all here.

After that line-up, if you are still reading, consider this: What is the cultural currency for most any teenager? What do our teenagers watch on their screens? For whom will a teenager drop everything? What is the one unifying true-north magnetic pull that spins the cultural needle for most any teenager? The answer is universal: *celebrities*. Celebrities hold the clout, set the style norms, dictate behavioral trends, and are the influencers for youth culture. What stories interest most any teenager? *Celebrity stories*. Bingo! This book uses short celebrity stories (the people whom our culture values most)—one after another—to teach life lessons. The stories are about celebrities; the lessons are from us.

Each celebrity story illustrates a monumentally *stupid behavior*. The lesson is to avoid that stupid behavior and its consequences. The fewer stupid things kids do, the more likely they will reach stable adulthood. It's not complicated.

To avoid being preachy, this book solicits reader participation. After each celebrity story, we turn the pen over to a member of the youth culture (Meggie) for her point of view. She reviews and grades each celebrity story, and the lesson attached to it.

Discussion questions follow each celebrity story, inviting more reader input (and sometimes hostility). Some celebrity stories leave a mark; others get nothing but an eye roll or maybe an outright F. Be forewarned, there is no grading curve when trying to influence youth culture. Readers may find Meggie's reviews (a.k.a. dad beatdowns) or the discussion questions superior to the celebrity stories themselves. And that is just fine with us. It's time to meet our youth reviewer-in-chief, Meggie.

• INTRODUCING MEGGIE'S TAKE •

Hey, readers! My name is Meggie, and my dad is the author. When Dad first told me he was writing a book on parenting, I have to admit, I was pretty skeptical. Once I started reading the drafts, I realized that if he ever wanted kids and parents to read the book together, he would have to include the kid perspective too. No kid I know wants to sit through a lecture from their parents without having a say. I know I don't speak for all kids, but I wanted "Meggie's Take" to be a way for kids to get a say in the process. Whether or not you agree with what I have to say or the grade I assign to each celebrity story, I hope that Meggie's Take will help springboard conversations between kids and parents, or at least help both parties see things from a different perspective. Dad challenged me to be brutally honest while writing, so I didn't pull any punches. Look out for Meggie's Take at the end of each section, and thanks for reading!

CONTENT WARNING

We don't dodge the hot-button issues facing today's teenagers. The celebrity stories include the usual suspects of alcohol, drugs, sex, relationships, sexting, HIV, gun violence, and pornography (all in a PG-13 manner). If we wish to pretend that our teenagers don't face these real-world issues, then close this book and turn on the Hallmark Channel.

DISCLAIMERS

This book makes many big claims and small suggestions.

Know this: We may be *wrong!* Really wrong.

There are no guarantees. Children born of the same parents, raised in the same home, nurtured in the same way, over the same time span often have wildly different life outcomes. It happens so often, there is a term for it: being the "black sheep" of the family. It's such a terrible label, but we all know what it means. There are terrific citizens who had lousy fathers (think Abraham Lincoln or Truett Cathy of Chick-fil-A) and lousy citizens who had upstanding dads (think serial killers Ted Kaczynski Jr. and Ted Bundy). That's just how it goes.

Children are complex. Family dynamics are complex. Good *parental inputs* (whatever that means) do not lead to good *child outcomes* (whatever that means) in a straight-line fashion. The most that can be said is good parental inputs only increase the likelihood of good child outcomes. And truth be told, probably not by much. Good parenting nudges against the child's natural baseline.

The inverse is also true but more severely so. Bad parental inputs (i.e. parental malpractice) increase the likelihood of bad child outcomes. But bad parenting doesn't just nudge, it shoves against the child's natural baseline. Bad parenting is much more likely to lead to bad child outcomes than good parenting is to lead to good child outcomes. Simply put, when it comes to parenting, it is easier to break than build. Therefore, we should always remember the parental Hippocratic oath: (1) Be humble, and (2) do no harm.

With the disclaimers out of the way, it's time to advance our big claims. Daniel Kahneman, a Nobel Laureate and influential psychologist, says it's necessary to make big claims—overpromising claims—in order to spark initial enthusiasm for any project and bust through the status-quo inertia.[1] If a social scientist or academic presented how hard long-term behavior change is to achieve, no personal-development book would ever be written or read. Therefore, we start with Kahneman's premise of being "unrealistically optimistic" that something in this book will assist in raising stable children and maybe even improve our own lives too.

But we may be wrong, so read and implement what you choose. Ignore and discard what you choose. Treat everything going forward as nothing but unproven suggestions. Before making suggestions, we begin with a threshold question from mega-celebrity Angelina Jolie: Are dads even necessary to raise stable children?

THE WISDOM OF ANGELINA JOLIE: ARE DADS EVEN NECESSARY?

> *It had never crossed my mind that [my son]*
> *Mad was going to need a father.*
> —Angelina Jolie (2007)

In 2002, while still married to Billy Bob Thornton, Angelina Jolie adopted her first child, Maddox. Within a year, Jolie filed for a divorce from Thornton. By 2005, Jolie, a single parent, was dating Brad Pitt. It was while dating Pitt that she recounted to *Vogue* magazine:

"There was a coming together of him [Maddox] and Brad. It's a big thing to bring together a child and a father. It had never crossed my mind that Mad was going to need a father—certainly not that it would be this man I just met."[2]

After nearly a decade together, Pitt and Jolie made it official and married on August 23, 2014, in the presence of their six children. Twenty-five months later, on September 19, 2016, Jolie filed for a divorce from Pitt.

Jolie's popularity has not wavered. In a 2018 YouGov survey across thirty-five countries, Jolie was ranked as the most admired woman in the WORLD![3] (Michelle Obama was second.) Yet in 2007, as the single parent of Maddox, it never crossed Jolie's mind that he would need a father. What an honest and sad admission. That is the celebrity culture in a story. Jolie is not alone, as evidenced by the culture voting her the most admired female in the world.

The good news is that most of us believe that fathers are useful. Let's begin with Part I encouraging our children to follow us Disappearing Dads with a secular message in order to be stable and modestly productive adults.

• PART I •

FOLLOW ME: THE DISAPPEARING DAD UNDER THE SUN

We are all Disappearing Dads—physical beings pulled by the culture and subject to the life cycle. We live, work, and play in the physical world—the world *under the sun*. Our feet are firmly on the ground, heads down and on task. If lucky, we get about fifty years to do the dad thing.

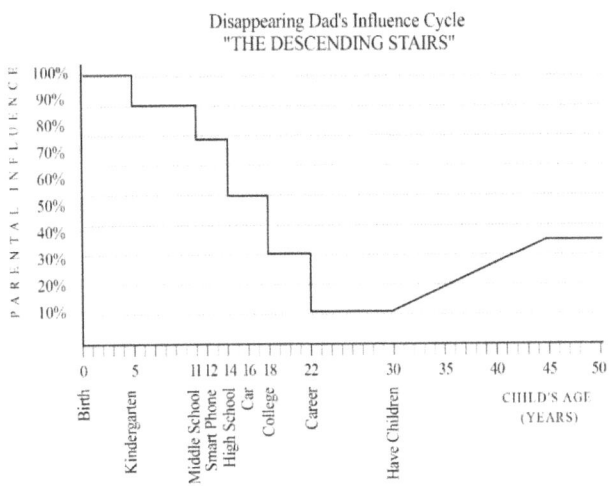

Though studies vary, the average life expectancy for a male in the US is seventy-seven years.[4] To make the math easy, assume our first child comes along when we are twenty-seven years old. That means we have fifty years to positively influence our children toward stable and productive lives.

The clock is ticking, and many of us are well into the third quarter of play and disappearing daily. Get over it. The final Disappearing Dad phase is when our children take away the car keys and move us into the nearby "retirement community." We then pass from Disappearing Dad to newly minted ancestor. Before that happens, let's share a few celebrity stories that will help keep our kids alive, a prerequisite to a stable and productive life.

• CHAPTER 1 •

THE CHILDHOOD DEADLY DECISIONS

I feel that if the kids are still alive when my husband gets home from work, then hey, I've done my job.
—Roseanne Barr

Roseanne Barr's joke about keeping kids alive is funny—until tragedy strikes. Teenagers just think differently. They think they are invincible and are going to live forever, or at least until thirty, which is forever in their world. The thought that someday they might be forty or even fifty years old is like saying little green Martians live next door, an incomprehensible concept from a faraway fantasy world. Against this mindset, try telling your teenagers that they are just one stupid decision away from *death*. That if they make one of these stupid, deadly decisions, they will be a "one-and-done" teenager. The predictable response (if you get one at all): "Yeah, right. Whatever."

Teenagers never think that death will visit them. It simply does not compute. (As an aside, neither do adults; incredibly, less than half of American adults have a will.[5]) There is not a teenager in America who woke up this morning saying, "Today is the day. I'm going to make a stupid decision and be dead before lunch." The truth is that *we agree* with our teenagers, if we think about it at all. We're all pretty good at believing that our kids are basically good and make safer decisions than the other kids at the bus stop. Besides, for the overwhelming supermajority, Roseanne Barr is right: Our kids are alive when we return home from work. We all believe that stupid decisions that can kill teenagers won't happen to our kids. Sure, we frequently hear about teenage deaths from our news feeds and TV, but it's not our story—it is always someone else's. And you know what? We're right. BIG TIME! It is highly, highly unlikely that any of our kids will die from making a stupid decision. That is great news and the reason we can laugh at Roseanne Barr's joke. The statistics are encouraging, provided you're in the 99 percent breathing group.

The world loses 1.2 million adolescents a year, largely from preventable causes, according to a global World Health Organization study released in May 2017.[6] An average of 16,375 teenagers in the twelve-through-nineteen age range died annually in the United States from 1999 to 2006, according to the Centers for Disease Control and Prevention.[7] This is less than 1 percent of all deaths that occur every year in the United States. The five leading causes of death among teenagers are accidents (unintentional injuries), homicide, suicide, cancer, and heart disease.[8] Accidents account for nearly half of all teenage deaths.[9] As a category of accidents, car fatalities were the leading cause of death to teens, representing over one-third of all deaths.[10]

In doing the grisly math, a 1 percent teenage death rate still represents 7,860 *preventable* deaths (i.e. 16,375 teenage deaths x 48 percent "unintentional" injuries) annually. And these numbers are before the opioid crisis that has decimated our youth. Compare that against Grandpa. In 2014, heart disease took 614,348 seniors (seventy-eight times the rate of teenager-preventable deaths).[11] Maybe we should spend more time making sure Grandpa takes his heart medicine than worrying about our teenagers. Statistically, we should. But as dads, the goal is to make sure our teenagers are part of the senior, not teenager, mortality statistics.

For our teenagers, death is a reverse lottery ticket—extremely rare but deadly to the holder. Consider this: Today, twenty-one US teenagers (i.e. 7,860 preventable deaths divided by 365 days) died from a preventable death. Tomorrow, another twenty-one will have their lottery tickets called. By week's end, 147 teenagers will be dead. The cycle repeats every week.

But it won't be our kids, right? It won't be our story, right? Not to sound cold, but that is our thinking. When it comes to our kids, we're not interested in risk management; we prefer risk elimination. But how? By convincing our children that if bad things can happen to celebrities—role models and influencers in their world—then bad things can happen to them too. If it is possible that teenagers can learn from the mistakes of others (admittedly a shaky premise), then let us begin by presenting the deadly decisions to coincide with the five leading causes of death among teenagers: accidents (unintentional injuries), homicide, suicide, cancer, and disease. As the celebrities prove, all it takes is one—just one!—really stupid decision to join the teenage-mortality statistic club.

• #1 Teen Killer: Car Accidents •

Car wrecks are the leading killer of teenagers, representing over one-third of all teen deaths. Therefore, the first two celebrity stories address this reality.

1. ONE RIDE

Celebrity: Paul Walker, Actor

Tinseltown/Shuterstock.com

Story

Paul Walker was one of America's most beloved action-movie stars for his lead role as a street racer in The Fast and the Furious movie franchise. Perhaps that provided him with some confidence the night he got into a Porsche Carrera GT with Roger Rodas, a competitive race car driver, to have some fun on the back roads of Valencia, California, while returning from a charity event—only they didn't have fun; they hit a tree at high speed and were both killed in the fiery crash. Walker was just forty years old.

Paul Walker was at the top of his game. He had starred in multiple television shows and dozens of movies. The Fast and the Furious franchise was already a worldwide phenomenon, and he was in the process of filming the seventh movie, *Furious 7*. It would become Walker's highest-grossing film, and remains at this printing the sixth-highest-grossing movie of all time.[12] The vast majority of commercial films don't gross over $100 million, yet all seven of The Fast and the Furious movies easily exceeded that mark. With the exception of Star Wars, that is an unmatched record.

Having a leading role in such a prosperous franchise comes with a lot of perks. Walker was worth over $25 million.[13] That buys a lot of cars. Walker made his fortune doing what he loved. By all accounts, Walker and Rodas were great guys and skilled drivers. However, Rodas had a mixed record. Walker had recently loaned Rodas one of his personal cars to race in, because Rodas had crashed his car and needed one to finish a race. In addition to sharing his mutual love of high-speed cars, Rodas was Walker's financial adviser. Walker trusted Rodas with much more than his money on November 30, 2013. He trusted him behind the wheel, and it cost him his life.

Lesson

Paul Walker was a skilled driver, but he died as a *passenger*, his skills useless as Roger Rodas lost control and crashed—again. No alcohol or drugs were involved, just speed and daring.

There are simple lessons here.

Let's not put ourselves in dangerous situations where the margin between life and death is slim; it's never worth it. But if we're thrill junkies and must take on unnecessary risk (stupidly), then take that risk individually. Let's not put our earthly fate in the hands of someone else in such small-margin situations. We'll be the master of our own vainglory or demise.

Walker had everything except the steering wheel that could keep him alive. The actor who ruled the silver screen ended up helpless to someone else driving him into a tree.

In the climactic scene in *Fast & Furious 6*, Vin Diesel, while driving and chasing the bad guy, turns to passenger Walker and says, "Ride or die, remember?" Walker affirms, "Ride or die," and they speed off to get the bad guy. Life sometimes imitates art. In Walker's case, the more accurate quote would be ride *and* die.

The upshot: Don't be a passenger in the car or in life. Take the wheel and drive your own destiny.

• MEGGIE'S TAKE •

Growing up, it annoyed me when my parents always wanted to know when I was riding in someone else's car and who was driving that car. I told my parents that my friends were responsible, and I wouldn't ride with them if they were bad drivers. My parents are kind of like those driver-education videos: They depict the worst-case scenario—usually death—and dramatize risk. To be fair, though, dying in a car accident from stupidity alone would be an epically disappointing way to go. And, I would never want my parents to feel responsible because they let me drive with a friend who was dangerous and got us killed.

I'll keep rolling my eyes when my parents worry about driving, but I get it. When you hear stories like Paul Walker's, it makes sense why parents question us anytime we go somewhere.

Grade: A

DISCUSSION QUESTIONS
(Child leads discussion.)

1. How well has Dad covered this lesson before?
2. Does Dad practice what he preaches regarding this lesson, or is he a hypocrite?
3. Does this lesson mean you should always try to be the driver if you're going somewhere with friends?
4. How can you know if you're in a dangerous situation and need to do something about it?
5. What would/should you do if you find yourself as a passenger in a dangerous situation?

NOTES:

2. ONE TEXT

Celebrity: Dr. Frank Ryan, Plastic Surgeon to the Stars

Story

Dr. Frank Ryan was a celebrity plastic surgeon and reworked the faces and bodies of many Hollywood stars. Ryan is a stark reminder of the dangers of texting, as he was reportedly tweeting about his dog just before his car plunged off a cliff in Malibu, California.

Ryan was known for performing multiple plastic-surgery procedures on celebrities, including Lorenzo Lamas, Heidi Montag, Gene Simmons, Shannon Tweed, Shauna Sand, Vince Neil, Adrianne Curry, Janice Dickinson, and many others. His most famous client, reality star Heidi Montag of MTV's *The Hills*, infamously underwent ten surgeries in one day, including a chin reduction, breast augmentation, butt augmentation, and a second nose job.

On August 16, 2010, at about 4:30 p.m., Ryan drove his car off the side of the twisty Pacific Coast Highway, and the vehicle landed on its roof. Lifeguards initially tried to help him. Ryan was trapped in the vehicle and had major head injuries. His dog, Jill, was thrown out of the vehicle, but survived with some minor injuries. On Ryan's social media, the last post reads, "After 25 years of driving by, I finally hiked to the top of the giant sand dune on the [Pacific Coast Highway] west of Malibu. Much harder than it looks! Whew!"[14] That missive was followed by a photo of Jill looking out at the Pacific Ocean with the caption, "Border collie Jill surveying the view from atop the sand dune."[15]

Each day in the United States, approximately nine people are killed and more than a thousand injured in crashes that are reported to involve a distracted driver, finds the CDC.[16] Teen drivers, ages fifteen through nineteen, are the largest proportion of drivers involved in fatal crashes.[17] Ten percent of all drivers in this age group involved in fatal crashes were reported as distracted at the time of the crash, reports the National Highway Traffic Safety Administration.[18]

According to a AAA poll, 94 percent of teen drivers acknowledge the dangers of texting and driving, but 35 percent admit to doing it anyway.[19]

Lesson

Dr. Ryan was a successful, admired Hollywood plastic surgeon who frequently appeared on major talk shows with his celebrity clients. Tweeting while behind the wheel cost him everything. If you are texting (or tweeting) while driving, you are not focused on the road and are putting yourself, your passengers, and other drivers at risk. At fifty-five miles per hour, a vehicle travels at eighty feet per second. So, taking your eyes off the road for a mere four seconds to read and reply to a text translates to your vehicle traveling 320 feet, or 106 yards—longer than a football field. A lot can happen over the span of a football field.

The upshot: Don't make the same mistake Ryan made. Keep your smartphone tucked away when you are driving. No status update is worth your life.

• MEGGIE'S TAKE •

Everyone knows how dangerous texting and driving is, yet we keep doing it because it seems unlikely that anything will actually happen to us. *It happens to other people, but not me, right?*

We have an invincibility complex, and it's difficult to shake. I get it. I am definitely guilty of texting and driving. How do you stop? The only way I know how (besides just having self-control, of course) is to put your phone in the trunk or the backseat. But there's a lot of excuses—some of them pretty good—that support having your phone in the front of the car with you. What if someone calls and it's an emergency? What if you get pinned under your truck and no one sees you, and the only way you can save yourself is to wriggle in such a way that Siri turns on in your back pocket and you can call 911? (Yep, that actually happened.[20]) I guess it's back to having self-control, then. Don't forget about other distractors, like changing the radio, talking on the phone (even if it's hands-free), or chatting with the passengers in your car. The bottom line: You have to know yourself. If you can't handle extra stimulants while you're driving, ask your passengers to talk among themselves instead of to you. Let the person in the passenger seat handle radio changes, and don't take calls. On the other hand, if you feel comfortable, I think it's totally fine to chat with your passengers. Just know yourself and your own ability to concentrate. Distracted driving is the issue, and if talking to your sister in the front seat doesn't distract you from the road, then I say go for it.

Grade: B

DISCUSSION QUESTIONS
(Child leads discussion.)

1. How well has Dad covered this lesson before?
2. Does Dad practice what he preaches regarding this lesson, or is he a hypocrite?
3. Why do you personally text and drive?
4. If you text and drive, what would it actually take for you to stop?
5. Would you feel comfortable asking your passengers to do something differently if they were distracting you?

NOTES:

• #2 Teen Killer: Homicides •

Homicides are the second-leading killer of teenagers.[21]

3. ONE GUN

Celebrity: Tupac Shakur, Rapper

Moviestore Collection/Alamy Stock Photo

Story

Hip-hop legend Tupac Shakur was born in East Harlem on June 16, 1971. He grew up on the rough streets of New York, Baltimore, and Compton, California. His mother, Afeni Shakur, was an active member of the Black Panther Party.

Shakur began his career using his music to share the struggles and injustices of many African Americans. The rapper and actor exemplified the 1990s image of gangsta rap, a style of hip-hop reflecting the violent lifestyles of inner-city youth.

Known by the stage names Tupac, 2Pac, and Makaveli, Shakur sold seventy-five million albums by the time of his death at age twenty-five, making him one of the top-selling artists of all time.[22] He was the victim of gun violence two different times in the 1990s, including in 1994, when he was shot and robbed as he was leaving Quad Studios in Manhattan. He was shot five times, and the assailants stole $40,000 in jewelry. Two years later, in 1996, he died from gunshot wounds received in another incident.

In 1995, Tupac signed with Death Row Records, and the label chief, Suge Knight, was known to be involved with a Los Angeles–based street gang. Knight was with Shakur on September 7, 1996, to watch a Mike Tyson fight at the MGM Grand Las Vegas. After leaving the fight, one of Knight's associates spotted Orlando "Baby Lane" Anderson, a member from another gang. A fight broke out, and Knight and members of his entourage were in the middle of it.

Later, as the car that Shakur was sharing with Knight stopped at a red light, a shooter from an adjacent car aimed out a back window and fired thirteen shots, hitting Shakur in the hand, pelvis, and chest, and also wounding Knight.[23] Chris Carroll, a retired sergeant with the Las Vegas Metropolitan Police Department, was the first officer to get to the dying Shakur. Shakur did not cooperate. As he was dying on the Las Vegas street, Carrol asked him, "Who shot you?" Shakur took a breath and responded, "F*** you!" Those were his last words.[24]

While Knight survived, Shakur died six days later. His murder has not been officially solved, but investigators with the Compton Police Department and the Las Vegas Metropolitan Police Department investigated Orlando Anderson as a possible suspect. In addition, Keefe D. Davis, Anderson's uncle and one of the alleged occupants of the car that approached Shakur on that fateful night, pinpointed his nephew as the trigger man.[25] But the truth of Davis' statements has been questioned and Anderson was never charged. Anderson died in Compton from a gunshot wound in 1998.

Lesson

This sad story highlights the deadly dangers of gangs and guns, which have contributed to a homicide rate among adolescents and young adults that is higher than any other age group.[26]

First, let's talk gangs. Some thirty-three thousand violent street gangs, motorcycle gangs, and prison gangs with about 1.4 million members are criminally active in the US and Puerto Rico today, according to the FBI.[27] Many are sophisticated and well organized; all use violence to control neighborhoods and boost their illegal money-making activities, which include robbery, drug and gun trafficking, prostitution and human trafficking, and fraud. Many gang members continue to commit crimes after being sent to jail.

Second, let's talk guns. A rash of mass shootings continues to plague our country, from the slaughter of fifty-eight people at the Route 91 Harvest Festival in Las Vegas in October 2017 to the killing of seventeen students at Marjory Stoneman Douglas High School in Parkland, Florida, in February 2018. But those senseless deaths pale numerically to what goes on every day in the big cities of America. The city of Chicago is the poster child for gun violence. According to the *Washington Post*,[28] the shootings and deaths in Chicago alone included:

Year	Shootings	Deaths from Shootings
2016	3,550	771
2017	2,785	650

The gun violence in Chicago is staggering. In the Parkland, Florida, 2018 high school mass shooting, seventeen lives were snuffed out. In Chicago, during the past two years, the average was 263 shootings that killed fifty-nine people *every month*, or more than three times the loss in Parkland, Florida. In 2016, shootings claimed more than thirty-eight thousand lives in the US, four thousand more than 2015. Nearly one-third were gun-related homicides.[29]

These are the facts. But before any of us "gun dads" start to mount a rebuttal, *relax*. This book is about kids, not guns. It is not a political manifesto and does not call for the repeal of the Second Amendment or the abolition of handguns. What the Shakur story and these statistics do prove beyond doubt is that guns are not toys to be played with; they are to be properly secured so that our teens can't get to them outside our presence. Second, our teenagers should have a healthy fear of persons who possess guns. If our children are to be around guns and hunting, they need to be trained in proper gun use and safety. If they find themselves in a situation where guns are being used improperly, then they need to exit pronto and look for a new group of friends.

The upshot: In the wrong hands, at the wrong time, tragic outcomes occur. A gun knows no race, creed, fame, or family when it's handled by a person willing to use it to destroy.

• MEGGIE'S TAKE •

I don't have much to say here. I'm intentionally not going to comment on the politics of guns and gun ownership in the US. That is a whole other can of worms. Here's what I'll say: Guns are dangerous; don't mess with them. If there are guns around, get out. End of story.

Grade: B

DISCUSSION QUESTIONS
(Child leads discussion.)

1. How well has Dad covered this lesson before?
2. Does Dad practice what he preaches regarding this lesson, or is he a hypocrite?
3. What do you think about gun rights in the United States right now?
4. Have you been at all influenced by guns or gangs? If so, how?
5. Is this a topic you and your friends talk about?

NOTES:

4. ONE HIT: STREET DRUG (COCAINE AND HEROIN) AND PRESCRIPTION DRUG (OPIATES) CRISES

Celebrity: Len Bias, Basketball Star

Story

On June 17, 1986, basketball player Len Bias was drafted in the first round by the Boston Celtics, the team that included Hall of Famers Larry Bird and Kevin McHale. He was supposed to extend the Boston basketball dynasty another decade, but two days later, Len Bias was dead of a cocaine overdose. He was twenty-two years old. He was one of the best college-basketball players ever. He was compared to Michael Jordan, except Bias was taller and stronger. Legendary Duke basketball coach Mike Krzyzewski put it this way: "And in that time, there have been two opposing players who have really stood out: Michael Jordan and Len Bias. I consider a playmaker as someone who can do things others can't, the way Jordan did. Bias was like that."[30] The day after Bias was drafted in New York, he went to Boston to discuss a $1.6 million endorsement deal with Reebok. After agreeing to the deal, Bias visited his family near his college campus at the University of Maryland, where he played college basketball and was loved by thousands of fans. Late on the night of June 18, Bias decided to go back to his dorm at the University of Maryland. After circulating between parties and his dorm in the early morning of June 19, Bias ended up back in his dorm with a few of his close friends. They decided to ingest cocaine—the last conscious decision Bias made. He started having seizures and died. A few hours of using cocaine reduced a six-foot-eight, 210-pound, robust figure of pure muscle, athleticism, and energetic youth to a limp, lifeless body.

Something like this was not supposed to happen. As detailed in "The Day Innocence Died" by Michael Weinreb of ESPN, Larry Bird, the previous year's NBA Most Valuable Player, called the news "one of the cruelest things I've ever heard."[31] Bias is remembered for who he could have been. To die so young is always tragic, but to leave so much potential behind is even more heartbreaking.

Lesson

Perhaps the lesson depends on your viewpoint. Again, as detailed in "The Day Innocence Died," different people took away different lessons from Bias' death. Some compared his death to the death of Christ, while others said he was just another guy who took cocaine and died.

For Children: "Not Me" Syndrome

As Meggie has confirmed, too many of our children believe they are invincible. Those that binge drink and take drugs do not believe their actions will lead to personal destruction, especially death. The "Not Me" syndrome is statistically correct; the overwhelming majority of teen drug users don't die or inflict permanent damage upon their lives. But for those who are not invincible, the consequences are fatal.

Sadly, there is no shortage of celebrity deaths due to drugs and alcohol abuse to rebut the "Not Me" syndrome.

THE SUPER DAD MYTH • 21

1977	Elvis Presley	Multiple prescription drugs, including codeine
1982	John Belushi	Heroin and cocaine
1997	Chris Farley	Cocaine and morphine
2008	Heath Ledger	Multiple prescription drugs, including opiates
2009	Michael Jackson	Propofol and benzodiazepine
2012	Whitney Houston	Cocaine
2016	Prince	Fentanyl

For this section, we picked Len Bias to focus on not because he was famous, but because he wasn't—and should have been. He died more than a decade before today's teenagers were born. That is the lesson. You can literally be the next Michael Jordan megastar but be destroyed by drugs, your legacy and name lost to future generations.

For Dads: "Not My Kid" Syndrome

The flip side of our kids' "Not Me" syndrome is the "Not My Kid" dad syndrome. Too many of us think the drug crisis will not hit our homes.

Eric Bolling, former Fox television personality and best-selling author, never thought the opioid crisis would touch his family. Then he got the phone call. His son, Eric Chase, died the first week of his sophomore year at the University of Colorado from an opioid overdose. Bolling said, "We never saw it coming, never thought we'd get that call." Bolling shared his story at the 2018 Opioids Summit at the White House. His advice? "The 'Not My Kid' syndrome is terrible. 'Not My Kid' syndrome is a killer."[32]

He advocated sitting down with our children and having the drug-and-alcohol discussion. To get more involved in their day-to-day activities. To find out who they are hanging out with and what they are spending money on. In the end, it's all about being less engaged in our own lives and more engaged in theirs.

Will that be enough? It is hard to know. Sometimes even the best parental efforts can't stop that call from coming. That is the insidious nature of the current opioid crisis and drug addiction.

> • MEGGIE'S TAKE •
>
> Well, that was terrifying. It's true—I've never even heard of Len Bias. If your intent with that lesson was to make sure I never do drugs, Dad, I think it's working. The idea of dying so young and suddenly is bad enough; the idea of having so much potential and still no one remembering you? Horrible.
>
> Grade: A

DISCUSSION QUESTIONS
(Child leads discussion.)

1. How well has Dad covered this lesson before?
2. Does Dad practice what he preaches regarding this lesson, or is he a hypocrite?
3. What kind of impact do you want to leave on the world?
4. How important is the future to you?
5. What would you feel comfortable doing if you found yourself in a situation that might become dangerous?

NOTES:

5. ONE PUNCH

Celebrity: Ray Rice, Star NFL Football Player

Story

On February 14, 2014, Ray Rice was a three-time Pro Bowl NFL running back, a Super Bowl champion the year before, the pride of the Baltimore Ravens, and a celebrity on top of the world. The next day, Rice was arrested for assaulting his girlfriend at an Atlantic City casino. He was twenty-seven years old, and his world, as he knew it, was over. News broke the next evening that Rice and his then-girlfriend (now wife) Janay Palmer had both been arrested on assault charges. A publicly released video showed Rice dragging his unconscious girlfriend out of an elevator into an Atlantic City casino lobby. In the next few months, Rice would be indicted on aggravated-assault charges, with the charges against his girlfriend being dropped.

Ultimately, Rice received a two-game suspension by NFL Commissioner Roger Goodell. The Ravens organization spoke up for Ray's character, as did John Harbaugh, head coach of the Ravens. Even his girlfriend spoke up for him, saying that the incident in the elevator was "a one-time thing."[33] Many significant people took Rice's side, and he allowed them to do so.

Then, in late summer of the same year, the video from *inside* the elevator surfaced. This new video showed Rice knocking Janay out with one punch. Rice was immediately cut by the Ravens and suspended indefinitely by the NFL. A scandal arose alleging that the NFL had seen the video before it was released to the public. The NFL was forced to create a new domestic-violence policy and admit they got Rice's initial punishment wrong.

Rice thought his indefinite NFL suspension unfair, and he appealed it. A federal judge overturned his indefinite suspension, as the NFL had put Rice into what is legally known as double jeopardy, being punished for the same crime twice. Yet through this, Roger Goodell testified that Ray Rice had, in fact, lied to him about what happened in the elevator.

On the critical question about what Rice had told Goodell about the incident, the commissioner testified that Rice had said he "slapped" his fiancée and had "minimized the impact of the physical contact" during the June 16 meeting. Goodell testified Rice specifically implied that it was not the blow that did any damage, it was actually the fact that she fell and knocked herself out.[34]

Even though Rice was eligible to sign with a team immediately after the ruling, no team has offered him a contract—almost four years later. Based on the NFL's reputation for being forgiving of players who commit crimes, one could conclude that Rice's continued lack of a job is due as much to his deception as it is to his punch.

On average, nearly twenty people per minute are physically abused by an intimate partner in the United States, according to statistics from National Coalition Against Domestic Violence.[35] In one year, this equates to more than ten million women and men.

More than half of female homicide victims are killed in intimate-partner violence, according to the CDC.[36] The study of deaths of women from intimate partners from 2003 to 2014 found that more than 55 percent of the deaths were related to partner violence.[37] Approximately one-third of female homicide victims were eighteen to twenty-nine years of age, while black and Native American/Alaskan Native women were more than twice as likely to be victims than other races.[38]

Lesson

Fortunately for all involved, Rice's punch didn't kill Janay Palmer, but it could have. It certainly killed his career. And while the NFL has had its share of high-profile domestic-violence incidents in the years since Rice's assault of Palmer, none have been as scrutinized or received more attention. Many commentators believe that is because Rice's incident was the first time we actually saw the assault happen.

Obviously, domestic abuse is wrong. Being physically abusive can ruin your reputation and your career. As night follows day, aggressors almost always try to cover up their misdeed by lying and enlisting others as allies to vouch for their character. Isn't that what happened here? Palmer said Rice's punch was a "one-time thing." Even if you believe that, don't be deceived that the "one punch" was Rice's only misdeed. It wasn't. Rice lied about it. He lied to his team, his coach, his fans, and the National Football League. He then enlisted others, including his coach and teammates, to speak out on his behalf, without giving them the full picture of what had happened *inside* the elevator, to minimize the damage to his reputation with the NFL and the public. He hoped that doing so would allow him to continue his all-star football career.

We live in a forgiving culture that welcomes redemptive comeback stories . . . *most of the time.* Janay Palmer forgave Rice and even married him. Should the public do likewise? The NFL passed. Rice was radioactive to the NFL, advertisers, media outlets, and other high-profile employers. If Rice had come clean from the beginning and not lied about the first misdeed, would he be viewed differently? Would he have gotten a shot to play in the NFL again, or is the elevator knockout-punch video just too severe, too unforgivable, and a permanent stumbling block to cultural forgiveness? There's no way to know, but one thing is clear: Physical violence and abuse almost always lead to serial dishonesty and, in turn, character ruin. Depravity begets depravity.

• MEGGIE'S TAKE •

When it comes to stories of violence and deception, I really don't have any sort of rebuttal to offer. Those things are wrong. It's sad that Rice's career was ruined, but at the same time, consequences are a very real and important thing. One thing I took away from this story is that people are more forgiving of misdeeds if there isn't an attempt at cover-up. If you're going to try to lie about having done something, you better be darn sure there is no possible way that ANYONE will EVER find out about it. Good luck with that.

Grade: A-

DISCUSSION QUESTIONS
(Child leads discussion.)

1. How well has Dad covered this lesson before?
2. Does Dad practice what he preaches regarding this lesson, or is he a hypocrite?
3. At what point, if ever, should you stop forgiving someone?
4. If someone were violent toward you but then told you it would never happen again, what would you do?
5. Which do you find harder: confessing to a misdeed, or covering it up?

NOTES:

• **#3 Teen Killer: Suicide** •

6. ONE LIFE

Celebrity: Kurt Cobain, Singer

Story

Kurt Cobain was the lead singer for Nirvana, one of the most popular bands of the early 1990s. Nirvana put out several Billboard-topping songs, including "Smells Like Teen Spirit," "About a Girl," and "Come as You Are." He married singer Courtney Love and had a young daughter named Frances Bean. Despite his success, Cobain struggled with addiction throughout his life. On April 8, 1994, electrician Gary Smith arrived at Cobain's Seattle home to install new wiring. He discovered Cobain dead on the floor, killed by a self-inflicted gunshot wound, with a suicide note found near his body. At the time of his death, Cobain was worth an estimated $100 million.

That April, Cobain had entered and quickly left rehab to treat his heroin addiction, and his wife was unable to locate him. Cobain had taken his life. Kurt Cobain and Courtney Love were a strange couple. Love encouraged Cobain to use drugs. The two had frequently taken drugs together, even while Love was pregnant with their daughter, Frances Bean. In addition to a strong heroin addiction, Cobain also suffered from bipolar disorder, a family history of suicide, alcohol abuse, depression, and stomach problems. In his suicide note, Cobain wrote, "I can't stand the thought of Frances becoming the miserable, self-destructive, death rocker that I've become. [. . .] I don't have the passion anymore, and so remember, it's better to burn out than to fade away."

Lesson

The US suicide rate has surged to a thirty-year high. Suicide among girls ages ten to fourteen has spiked over the last eighteen years, while "there's been a shocking surge in children seventeen or under dying from self-inflicted gunshot wounds."[39]

Since 1999, suicide rates have risen in every age group except the elderly, according to the National Center for Health Statistics.[40] Suicide currently accounts for 11 percent of teenage deaths.[41] Consider the suicide deaths of comedian Robin Williams, film producer Tony Scott, and artist Vincent van Gogh. No one knows what causes a person to take his or her life, so we can't generalize about suicide. It's an extremely complicated and sensitive issue. There are no easy solutions, so we don't offer any.

But one possible takeaway from Cobain's story is the influence that others—mainly his wife—had on his "miserable, self-destructive" self. This was not a situation where Love was leading Cobain in a bad direction; he was already careening down a destructive path. They both had addictions. Yet *together*, their addictions became worse. They fed off each other, and the result was fatal for Cobain.

The influence of family and friends is important. We are (or soon become) *who* and *what* we choose to surround ourselves with daily. The power of association is overwhelming. If we choose to associate with gangs and guns, we will become gang members. If we choose to hang around with musicians and instruments, we will become band members. If we choose to be around conscientious students and homework, we will become successful students. The timeless lesson is that we generally become who and what we associate with, so we must choose wisely. Cobain chose to surround himself with a codependent spouse and drugs. He did not choose wisely.

• MEGGIE'S TAKE •

I hate to agree with my dad so much, but I think he's right about his point on who we surround ourselves with. I've seen over and over in my life how similar I become to my close friends. We even start talking like each other! There's a difference between being nice to people and condoning everything they do. Having friends who support you (and not your destructive habits) is key.

Grade: A

DISCUSSION QUESTIONS
(Child leads discussion.)

1. How well has Dad covered this lesson before?
2. Does Dad practice what he preaches regarding this lesson, or is he a hypocrite?
3. How are the people you're surrounding yourself with right now shaping you?
4. Have you ever seen yourself change to become more like someone else?
5. What can you do if you're worried about a friend being suicidal?

NOTES:

• #4 and #5 Teen Killers: Disease •

In reality, the number-four killer of teenagers is cancer and the number-five killer is heart disease, according to CDC statistics.[42] However, rather than focus on these specific diseases, the next stories will take on the topic of disease more broadly.

7. ONE SMOKE: LEGAL DRUGS (TOBACCO)

Celebrity: Patrick Swayze, Actor

Story

Actor, dancer, and singer/songwriter Patrick Swayze was a lifelong smoker. Two of his more famous acting roles included the 1987 hit *Dirty Dancing* and the 1990 romantic fantasy/crime thriller *Ghost*. Having gained fame with appearances in films like *The Outsiders* during the 1980s, Swayze became popular for playing tough guys and romantic male leads, gaining him a wide fan base with female audiences, and status as a teen idol and sex symbol. Unfortunately, pancreatic cancer took him on September 14, 2009. He was fifty-seven.

According to the CDC, tobacco use is the most consistent risk factor for pancreatic cancer. About 20 percent of all pancreatic cancer cases are attributable to cigarette smoking. Smokers are about two times more likely to develop pancreatic cancer than nonsmokers. Studies have shown that the risk for developing this type of cancer gets lower over time after you quit smoking.[43]

Swayze was a very athletic actor with a strong dance background. Born in Houston, Texas, in 1952, Swayze was the second child of Patsy Swayze, a choreographer, dance instructor, and dancer, and Jesse Wayne Swayze, an engineering draftsman. He had two younger brothers and two sisters. His mother raised him in the performance arts, and eventually he would go on to study ballet in New York. He enjoyed a very active lifestyle, but continued to smoke all through adulthood.

Swayze acknowledged that his lifetime of smoking "probably had something"[44] to do with causing his cancer. He also claimed he could've easily quit smoking after being diagnosed with pancreatic cancer in January of 2008, but he didn't—or perhaps couldn't. He continued to chain-smoke until the day he died. Some believe he smoked as many as sixty cigarettes per day. As for why he didn't stop smoking after his cancer diagnosis, he explained in a Barbara Walters interview, "Will stopping smoking now stop anything, change anything? No. When it looks like I may live longer than five minutes, I'll drop cigarettes like a hot potato."[45] Swayze was so caught up with not letting cancer change his life that he didn't even bother to change the part of his life he believed contributed to the cancer.

Lesson

A generation ago, slang for cigarettes was "coffin nails," an apt description. Smoking is blamed for about one in five deaths annually, or 1,300 deaths every day. On average, smokers die ten years earlier than nonsmokers.[46]

But teenagers are smarter now. The statistics show a massive reduction in teenage smoking, and not just a little, but by a lot. In fact, cigarette smoking among high school students is now the lowest it's ever been since the CDC started the National Youth Risk Behavior Survey. Just 10.8 percent of high schoolers smoked in 2015, compared with 15.7 percent in 2013. The high school smoking rate is now a third of what it was just twenty years ago. And in 2016, for the first time, both vaping and smoking rates went down, the CDC reported.[47]

"The decline in use of tobacco products was primarily driven by a drop in e-cigarette use among middle and high school students from 3 million in 2015 to just under 2.2 million in 2016," the CDC report stated. Kids are starting to understand the potential ramifications of smoking, which is good news. Hopefully this trend will continue, and one day the health effects of tobacco addiction in young people will be a nonissue.

But, for those rebels who have decided to take up smoking, here is the short lesson of what to expect. Young people who start smoking will become addicted to nicotine, putting them at risk of smoking for the rest of their lives. Even a cancer diagnosis may not keep the most addicted from their habit, as Patrick Swayze taught us.

Talk to a smoker, and inevitably stories of failed attempts to quit smoking will come up. Smoking is a dangerous game. If played, you will lose and die early. Smoking is suicide, slowly administered. A final note to all smokers: Enjoy your children to the fullest, because you won't be around to enjoy your grandchildren.

• MEGGIE'S TAKE •

Here's another example of our invincibility complex. Sure, smoking is bad for you and reduces your lifespan—blah, blah, blah. But adulthood feels so far off! You might as well enjoy life a little now, right? This is a mindset I think most of us have as kids and young adults. And before you are quick to judge people who smoke, think about the destructive habits you yourself have. There's a cool book called *The Power of Habit* by Charles Duhigg, which says you won't be able to get rid of a habit; you can only replace it with another one. I don't know a lot about nicotine addiction, so I'm sure it's a lot more complicated than that. Yet perhaps replacing a bad habit with a good one, in conjunction with proven methods of fighting addiction, can help you if you find yourself with a destructive habit, smoking or otherwise.

Grade: B

DISCUSSION QUESTIONS
(Child leads discussion.)

1. How well has Dad covered this lesson before?
2. Does Dad practice what he preaches regarding this lesson, or is he a hypocrite?
3. Are people who smoke considered "cool," in your experience?
4. Would you consider smoking to be a "rebel" move?
5. Do you have any habits you want to break?

NOTES:

8. ONE DRINK: LEGAL DRUGS (ALCOHOL AND ALCOHOLISM)

Celebrity: Amy Winehouse, Singer

Steven May/ Alamy Stock Photo

Story

Extraordinary artistic talent Amy Winehouse broke into the music business when a classmate passed her demo tape to a record label. The Londoner signed her first record deal as a jazz vocalist at sixteen years old. She swept the 2008 Grammy Awards, winning six Grammys, including Song of the Year and Album of the Year. Her songs "Back to Black," "You Know I'm No Good," and "Rehab" won her fame. Her unique blend of soul, jazz, and blues vocals differentiated her in a crowded music industry. Winehouse wrote "Rehab" based on her own struggles with drug and alcohol abuse. Many who were close to her say fame killed her.

"Fame came like a huge tidal wave," former Winehouse friend and manager Nick Shymansky said in an interview on MSNBC's *Morning Joe* after the release of *Amy*, the bio-documentary. "The fame came very, very quick and very strong," Shymansky said. "She got depressed, she got lost, she got into a bad crowd, started trying heavy drugs . . ."[48]

Director Asif Kapadia elaborated, "As she became mega-famous and a worldwide star . . . [it] got out of control. She couldn't control it. People around her maybe weren't experienced enough to control it."[49]

Winehouse was woefully unprepared for fame, writes clinical psychologist Donna Rockwell, PsyD, in her 2015 post "Amy Winehouse, the Reluctant Celebrity: A Parable on the Fatal Cost of Fame." Rockwell notes, "Fame objectifies the famous. While the spotlight grows brighter, a famous person's sense of self may actually fade. In short order, the overwhelming reality of the unrelenting glare of celebrity can leave the newly enthroned at a loss."[50] Winehouse was quoted as saying in the documentary, "If I could give it all back just to walk down the street with no hassles, I would do it."

In addition to a heroin addiction, which intensified by her two-year marriage to fellow addict Blake Fielder-Civil, Winehouse struggled with bulimia and alcoholism. These addictions hurt both her personal life and her professional career—Winehouse was booed off the stage during a shaky performance in Serbia in 2011.

In the spring of 2011, Winehouse went to rehab and attempted to become sober. However, one final relapse proved to be too much for her body, which was already weakened by bulimia. On July 23, 2011, Winehouse was dead in her London apartment with a blood alcohol concentration of 0.416. She was twenty-seven years old.

Lesson

Winehouse is a member of the "Forever 27 Club," which refers to the many rock 'n' roll artists whose lives were cut short by suicide or drug/alcohol overdoses at the age of twenty-seven. Members of the club include Kurt Cobain, Jimi Hendrix, Janis Joplin, and Jim Morrison. The members of this club demonstrate the fatal effect that alcohol or drug addiction can have on the lives of anyone. Their deaths drive home the danger of alcohol and drug abuse.

The members of the Forever 27 Club were not alone in their overdoses or in their addictions; they were surrounded by others who engaged in the same behavior. One thing our kids do very well is spot hypocrisy. If we preach to our children not to drink, but then we get drunk or comfortably numb on the weekends, then our message is dead. Don't bother. If alcohol is a stumbling block, then consider skipping this lesson rather than lose credibility concerning the other celebrity lessons in this book where our actions mirror our words.

> • MEGGIE'S TAKE •
>
> Amy Winehouse's death is a tragic story. I remember hearing about it in the news. But there's a difference between drinking and getting drunk. I know from talking with my friends that there are a lot of different ways parents deal with this issue. Some have their kids start drinking at home so that they can figure out their limits in a safe environment. Some parents expect their kids to never drink because they consider it to be "morally wrong," and think that their kids should agree. But the thing is, so many people in college don't find this reasoning to be enough, and they start drinking anyway.
>
> Here's what I think: If you want your kids to not drink at all, give them a better reason than just "It's wrong," or "We don't do it, which means we're setting a good example." That reasoning is no match for the vast majority of your kids' peers, who will find nothing wrong with drinking.
>
> If a kid has a good enough reason to not drink, they won't do it. Mom and Dad telling them simply "It's bad" will probably not be enough. On the other hand, if you can't give your child a good enough reason (or help them figure out that reason on their own), don't be naïve. Realize that they probably will drink, and help them figure out how to do it without ending up like Amy Winehouse.
>
> Grade: B-

DISCUSSION QUESTIONS
(Child leads discussion.)

1. How well has Dad covered this lesson before?
2. Does Dad practice what he preaches regarding this lesson, or is he a hypocrite?
3. What would be a strong motivation to make you not drink?
4. Where do you think the best environment is to figure out your limits?
5. What reasons have your parents given you to not drink?

NOTES:

• CHAPTER 2 •

THE CHILDHOOD DAMAGING DECISIONS

As we move away from "deadly decisions," the good news is that if our children elect to make the "damaging" decisions outlined in this chapter, they still get to live. They will be wounded, but not dead. This chapter illustrates celebrity cautionary tales that limit upward mobility, but redemption and comeback stories are still possible.

9. ONE ONE-NIGHT STAND AFTER ANOTHER (HIV)

Celebrity: Charlie Sheen, Actor

stocklight/Shutterstock.com

Story

Charlie Sheen, the Golden Globe-winning actor whose breakthrough role in Oliver Stone's *Platoon* led to multiple leading-man roles, was far removed from his teenage years when he contracted HIV. His off-screen antics with drugs, alcohol, and adult-film stars led him to a cult-celebrity status. In November 2015, he revealed he was HIV positive.

Sheen didn't learn from the lessons of other hard-living celebrities. Sheen went right down the same path, believing that it could never happen to him. Sometimes, education takes repetition.

The good news is that medicine and treatments have advanced to the point where people with HIV/AIDS can live long and productive lives. Thankfully, HIV is no longer the death sentence it once was, but a complete cure remains out of reach.

Yet Charlie Sheen still travels and parties. He has yet to turn his focus beyond himself. In contrast, Magic Johnson, while living with HIV for decades, has led an incredibly productive, successful, and inspiring life. Johnson and Sheen both thought it couldn't happen to them. They were all wrong.

Who amongst us will be wrong next?

> ### • MEGGIE'S TAKE •
>
> The problem here is that young people often have the feeling that nothing *that* bad is going to happen—and not just in their sexual lives. Sure, bad stuff happens to some people, but the odds of that happening to us are pretty low, right?
>
> Unfortunately (and I realize I'm being pessimistic here), I'm not sure how to combat this mindset. Once you've talked to your kid about using protection and maybe given them some statistics about STDs, there's little else you can do.
>
> Grade: B

DISCUSSION QUESTIONS
(Child leads discussion.)

1. How well has Dad covered this lesson before?
2. Does Dad practice what he preaches regarding this lesson, or is he a hypocrite?
3. What do you wish your parents had done differently in talking to you about sex?
4. What do you think is the most effective way to teach kids about the dangers of sex?
5. On a scale from one to ten, how uncomfortable do you feel right now?

NOTES:

10. ONE LIE

Celebrity: John Edwards, US Senator

Story

John Edwards had it all. A rich, successful attorney and highly respected politician, Edwards was a leader in the Democratic Party, a senator from North Carolina, the 2004 vice presidential candidate with John Kerry, and a presidential candidate in 2008. By all appearances, his marriage to Elizabeth Edwards seemed solid. She was his loyal partner and trusted adviser. Together, they had weathered the unthinkable: the loss of their sixteen-year-old son, Wade, in April 1996 after a tragic car accident, which the couple said brought them closer together.

Edwards had a good story, a good name, and was on the rise. And then came the cheating, the cheating denial, the mistress, the mistress denial, the love child, the love-child denial. Edwards tried to keep his footing atop a mountain of lies and deceit, but the mountain crumbled, and Edwards' fall was straight down.

Doctors diagnosed Elizabeth Edwards with breast cancer in 2004. The cancer went into remission, but never fully left her body. Meanwhile, Edwards wanted another shot at presidential politics. He announced his second presidential campaign in December of 2006. In the late summer and fall of that year, Edwards worked with a woman named Rielle Hunter, whom he met at a bar in New York. Hunter was an independent producer, and Edwards commissioned her to create several "webisodes" of himself on the campaign trail, paying her over $100,000 for her services.

Elizabeth's cancer returned in March of 2007, but she continued to campaign with Edwards as he raced toward the 2008 Democratic primary season. In July of 2007, they celebrated their thirtieth wedding anniversary. Then the news broke. After receiving a tip from one of Rielle Hunter's friends, the *National Enquirer* reported in October that Edwards was having an affair with an unnamed woman. Edwards immediately denied the report—and denied it repeatedly on the campaign trail. In December 2007, the *National Enquirer* reported that Edwards had a pregnant mistress, Rielle Hunter. Edwards again denied the claims, and suspended his presidential campaign in January of 2008 for unspecified reasons. Edwards endorsed Barack Obama in May of 2008.

On February 27, 2008, Frances Quinn Hunter was born to Rielle Hunter in California. A former aide to Edwards, Andrew Young, came forward as the father (another lie perpetuated by Edwards). However, the *National Enquirer* stuck with its story of Edwards being the father. It published another report in July that Edwards had met with Hunter and their baby in the Beverly Hilton Hotel in California. It included pictures of someone who looked like Edwards holding a baby. Edwards had, in fact, stayed in the hotel that night, which made the story even more convincing.

With all the mounting allegations and evidence of an affair and love child, Edwards decided to address the topic in an interview on NBC's *Nightline* news program. In the August 8, 2008, interview, Edwards admitted to having a "short" affair with Hunter, which he said he immediately told his wife about. Edwards claimed the affair ended in 2006, around the time he had stopped filming with Hunter. He then denied that Frances Hunter was his child.

Of course, even those who wanted to believe that Edwards was telling the truth about the baby had a hard time squaring his prior repeated denials (now recanted). He said he'd take a paternity test, but never committed to a date in the interview.

In February 2009, the US Department of Justice opened an investigation into Edwards' 2008 campaign's finances. Among the chief issues in the investigation were the legitimacy of Rielle Hunter's business relationship with Edwards during the campaign and the vast sums of money paid to her by the campaign. Edwards claimed it was all within the regulations. The case would later be dropped in 2012 due to a jury deadlock and a mistrial.

Elizabeth Edwards went on *The Oprah Winfrey Show* in 2009 to address the affair and John's alleged illegitimate child. She stated that she didn't know whether the child was his or not, stating, "I don't have any idea," which led to further public mistrust of John Edwards.

In January 2010, the truth came out. Threatened by the imminent publishing of a tell-all book from former aide Andrew Young, Edwards finally admitted that he fathered Frances Quinn Hunter. This revelation confirmed many lies. First, it meant Edwards was a prolific liar who would only tell the truth when all other options were exhausted. Second, he had cheated on his terminally ill, breast cancer-stricken wife. And finally, as if in a Shakespearean tragedy, he had deliberately denied his own child!

Lesson

Edwards denied his own child for political purposes. That is profoundly sad. There's only one thing that could have stopped Edwards from embarrassing himself and his family so badly: *honesty*. If you don't want to be worried about covering up a web of lies, don't lie in the first place. If you don't want to feel compelled to lie about something you did, don't do something you'll have to lie about later.

Dads, imagine being Frances Hunter and knowing your father purposefully denied you for two years. Talk about a rocky start to a relationship. Fortunately, the relationship between Edwards and Frances can be salvaged, and from news reports is already on the mend. Redemption stories are always possible. Unfortunately for Edwards, his wife died in 2010. Elizabeth Edwards died just in time to see all the lies uncovered and witness the federal investigation into the campaign for which she had worked so hard. Knowing your relationship with your spouse will never be the same again can't be useful when fighting cancer. You may not be a national figure with tabloids constantly on your tail, but spouses and kids are the best lie detectors in the world.

Lies beget more lies. As they multiply, they generally involve bringing others in to maintain the deceit. The truth is, lying controls you and can ruin your good name. Edwards is a perfect example of this.

Dads, again, we're on the hook for ensuring our kids are honest. If Junior comes home smelling like sex, weed, or alcohol, chances are Junior was around sex, weed, or alcohol. But what happens when Junior says, "Oh, that was just my friends," or "It wasn't me"? If we suspect something is up, we need to find out the truth, not look the other way. We need to engage and respond. Now, how effective our response is remains to be seen. Some teenagers just lose their way despite tremendous positive parental efforts, but let's not pretend that problems don't exist or hope this is just a phase that will pass. Maybe a good start would be to share a story about John Edwards or Len Bias. It couldn't hurt.

• MEGGIE'S TAKE •

Obviously, lying is a slippery slope. You shouldn't do it. But kids often lie when they feel like they don't have any other options. If your kid feels like you're unreasonable, then watch out. Kids are creative, which means they are extremely good at deceiving you. The harder you try to police them, the more they will try to wriggle out of your grasp. The more you act like you don't trust your kid, the more untrustworthy he or she will become.

So, what is to be done? All kids operate differently and have different motivations, but the thing that frustrated me as a kid was being told to do or not do something with no explanation as to why. A major theme in all my rebuttals so far has been the idea of giving your kids a good motivation for doing (or not doing) a certain thing. I think that applies here too.

If you tell your kid to do something "because I say so," then yeah, I guess that's your right. However, that will only add to a kid's frustrations and make them want to do the exact opposite of what you "say so." The message sent to the kid is that you don't value their opinion or thoughts about something, or even worse, that it's not worth your time to explain things to them. The "because I say so" reason only holds as long as you can enforce it. When your kid leaves for college and has no reason to do something except their mom "said so," good luck to you, Mom. You are treating your kid like a baby (at least in their mind), so they might as well act like one. If you never allow your kid to see his girlfriend, then unless he is just an incredible kid, he will probably go behind your back. Now, instead of controlling the situation by allowing them to see each other but putting in place proper constraints, you have zero control, no idea what your kid is doing, and no credibility in your own kid's eyes.

Grade: B-

DISCUSSION QUESTIONS
(Child leads discussion.)

1. How well has Dad covered this lesson before?
2. Does Dad practice what he preaches regarding this lesson, or is he a hypocrite?
3. Why do you think people lie?
4. Do you think your parents trust you? Do you think you deserve their trust?
5. Does the "because I say so" argument work for you?

NOTES:

11. ONE PREGNANCY

Celebrity: Bristol Palin, Public Figure

Story

Bristol Palin is the daughter of the 2008 Republican vice presidential nominee, Sarah Palin. She, her family, and much of her mother's political party were supporters of abstinence and opposed out-of-wedlock childbirths and teen pregnancies. Then, on September 1, 2008—just two months before the election—the Palins had an announcement: Bristol was pregnant.

A well-off child of privilege, Bristol met Levi Johnston at Wasilla High School, where he was a hockey player and an avid outdoorsman. Sometime around March of 2008, Bristol became pregnant. Exactly how and where it happened is uncertain, because the two have written opposing memoirs with very different accounts. Bristol claims she was on a camping trip with Levi and some friends when Levi got her drunk and took advantage of her. She claims she felt like her virginity had been "stolen" when she woke up and found out from her friends what had happened.[51] Levi alleges that the two had been having regular, consensual sexual relations while Bristol was on birth control, but she stopped taking it without telling him.[52] He continues to allege that she initially lied to him about the pregnancy, and only wanted to get pregnant because she was jealous of her mom's baby.[53]

Talk about two sides to a story. Either way, her parents found out that she was pregnant and announced the news to the national media. That is probably not the story that John McCain and Sarah Palin wanted to break in the final stretch of the presidential campaign.

One could expect the immediate aftermath. The national media reported the pregnancy, many political pundits on both sides called the Palins hypocrites, and the McCain-Palin campaign took a hit. Bristol gave birth to her baby, Tripp, in December of 2008. Bristol and Levi had intended to get married after learning about the pregnancy, but split up in March of 2009. A custody-and-child-support battle unfolded between the two. On the employment front, things turned upward for Bristol, as she was hired by the Candie's Foundation to promote awareness about teen pregnancy. She was paid $262,500 for speaking and public-service campaigns.[54] It seemed natural that someone who had been through a teen pregnancy should be one to speak out about it. That's how Bristol felt.

She felt so confident she had learned her lesson that in May 2009, when she was eighteen years old, she took a vow of abstinence, telling *In Touch* magazine, "I'm not going to have sex until I'm married; I can guarantee it."[55] You can guess the next part of the story. At twenty-four years old, Bristol was pregnant again. She had her second baby in December of 2015. By early 2016, Bristol was fighting Levi Johnston and Dakota Meyer, the "baby daddies," in court over child support and visitation rights. Bristol ended up marrying Meyer in the summer of 2016, and the following May they welcomed their second child (and Bristol's third).

In today's culture, the pregnancies kept Bristol ever-present in the tabloids and in the public eye. Take this test: Can you name any of Sarah Palin's other children? Which Palin child did the popular TV show *Dancing with the Stars* call to join the cast (twice, in seasons 11 and 15)? It was Bristol. In her unusual case, the multiple pregnancies made Bristol a "celebrity personality" (think Kim Kardashian) who is "famous for being famous." So far, she has parlayed it into a workable lifestyle. But time moves on, and unless *Dancing with the Stars* calls again, Bristol is back working as an assistant to a dermatologist in Anchorage, Alaska.

Our kids are not Bristol Palin because we're not celebrities. Since we don't garner national media attention, neither will our daughters, pregnant or not. There is no $262,500 abstinence-spokesperson job waiting. People won't pay $100,000 for the exclusive rights to the baby pictures. *Dancing with the Stars* won't be calling. There is no reality show waiting to follow our kids around with their little rascals in tow. On the contrary, teen pregnancy is usually a one-way ticket to poverty and dependence. The statistics are bleak. Over three-quarters of unmarried teen mothers begin receiving welfare within five years of the birth of their first child.[56] That is a staggering statistic. Also, they can typically kiss college goodbye. Bristol Palin never went to college and works in a doctor's office to provide for her family. That is probably better than most outcomes waiting for high school–educated single mothers. Following are the tough statistics for what life looks like for teenagers having babies.

Teens

- By age twenty-two, only around 50 percent of teen mothers have received a high school diploma, and only 30 percent have earned a general education development (GED) certificate, whereas 90 percent of women who did not give birth during adolescence receive a high school diploma.
- Only about 10 percent of teen mothers complete a two- or four-year college program.
- Teen fathers have a 25–30 percent lower probability of graduating from high school than teenage boys who are not fathers.
- The growth of single-parent families remains the most important reason for increased poverty among children over the last twenty years, as documented in the 1998 Economic Report of the President. Out-of-wedlock childbearing (as opposed to divorce) is currently the driving force behind the growth in the number of single parents, and half of first out-of-wedlock births are to teens. (Source: The National Campaign to Prevent Teen Pregnancy)[57]

Children

- Have a higher risk for low birth weight and infant mortality

- Have lower levels of emotional support and cognitive stimulation
- Are more likely to be incarcerated at some time during adolescence
- Have lower school achievement and are more likely to drop out of high school
- Are more likely to give birth as teens
- Are at greater risk for being unemployed or underemployed as young adults

    (Source: The National Campaign to Prevent Teen Pregnancy)[58]
- A child born to a teen mother who has not finished high school and is not married is nine times more likely to be poor than a child born to an adult who has finished high school and is married.

    (Source: The National Campaign to Prevent Teen Pregnancy)[59]

Teen pregnancy is deeply intertwined with poverty and a lack of education. Whether you believe teen pregnancies are caused by poverty and poor education or vice versa, the result is the same. Teens, males and females alike, who have children are less likely to earn a high school diploma and are much less likely to earn a college degree. Their children are more likely to live in poverty, and the cycle grinds on from one generation to the next.

Lesson

Giving birth to a child is a wonderful thing. All children are created in God's image and are to be given life and loved unconditionally. Welcoming a new life into the world is never bad and always a cause for celebration. There is dignity in life—all life. But there is another side to that coin. The lesson here is to simply wait and avoid being a parent while you are still a child. Being a teenager is hard. Being a parent is hard. Being a teenage parent is nearly impossible.

• MEGGIE'S TAKE •

You know what's unfair? It takes two people to get pregnant. Yet do you see who gets put in the public spotlight here? The woman. You see who is affected by most of the negative statistics cited above? Yep, the woman. That sucks.

One other thing. The fact that their daughter got pregnant shouldn't make the whole Palin family hypocrites. Your parents could do everything right, and you could still make a mistake. That sucks too. But don't try to blame your parents for mistakes you made yourself.

Grade: C

DISCUSSION QUESTIONS
(Child leads discussion.)

1. How well has Dad covered this lesson before?
2. Does Dad practice what he preaches regarding this lesson, or is he a hypocrite?
3. If you or your partner got pregnant, how do you think your parents would respond?
4. If you or your partner got pregnant, how do you think your friends would respond?
5. What would be the most compelling argument your parents could make against having premarital sex?

NOTES:

12. ONE EDUCATION

Celebrity: John Krasinski, Actor

Story

John Krasinski grew up with two parents and two brothers. He attended Newton South High School, a public high school in the suburbs of Boston. He had friends. He was on the cross-country team and the basketball team. By all accounts, Krasinski was a pretty good kid who made good decisions most of the time. His life continued upward after he got accepted into Brown University, where he excelled. He went into college expecting to become an English teacher, but like so many college students do, he changed his mind. He graduated with honors as a playwright in 2001.

While Krasinski was in college, he had the opportunity to intern at NBC working for *Late Night with Conan O'Brien*. Krasinski spent the first semester of his freshman year teaching English in Costa Rica. He got more volunteer experience in college when he was an assistant basketball coach at a grade school in Providence, Rhode Island, near Brown. He developed his character by devotion to his studies, experiential learning through work, and volunteering to enrich the lives of others in his community and abroad.

Was all this beneficial to Krasinski? You could say that. After college he went on to attend several top acting centers, something he could do because he had such a high-quality education. He worked as a waiter to support himself while he attended The Actors Center in New York. There, he got his first acting gigs, small roles in commercials and TV shows. For several years, he had small roles in relatively unknown films and a few TV shows. Krasinski landed his first major acting role in 2005, the role he is most famous for today: Jim Halpert in *The Office*. His leading role as Jim brought him nationwide fame as *The Office* gained popularity. As a member of the cast, Krasinski won two Screen Actors Guild Awards and was nominated for several others. He has been nominated for one Emmy Award and numerous other, less-well-known awards.

In 2010, he married actress Emily Blunt. Krasinski's success from *The Office* brought him several large movie roles, but he never left the show. After nine seasons, the hit series ended. Krasinski would later say this about it: "I was a waiter when I got the show. I was twenty-three years old. A decade of my life! Not only has it given me every opportunity in the business, but I wouldn't have met Emily. In a very big, existential way, it's the most important thing in my life."

The show brought him more than he had ever dreamed of. And Brown University brought him to the show.

Lesson

You may be wondering, *Where's the damaging decision here?* There isn't one. We threw you a curveball. Instead of having all the stories teach a lesson through a negative story, here we slip in a lesson through a positive story.

Krasinski was a good guy growing up, a guy many of us can relate to. Now he's worth millions. He has two daughters, a beautiful wife, fame, a home in Southern California, and is living the dream. He and his wife are involved with charitable work.

How did all this happen? It's simple: He got a great education, enriched his life through volunteer work and experiential learning, and made the most of his opportunities. He made *good decisions*, one after another.

Well done, Mr. Krasinski, for teaching, through example, that good decisions can lead to great outcomes. Class dismissed early!

• MEGGIE'S TAKE •

What a nice story. Who doesn't love Jim from *The Office*? Good for Krasinski, seriously. The problem is, this lesson section makes it sound so easy. Just make good decisions, kids! Sure, Krasinski made good decisions, but he also had some amazing opportunities and a fair amount of luck. Not everyone has the same opportunities.

I'm not trying to minimize Krasinski and his accomplishments. Just don't get trapped into being self-congratulatory without realizing the ways you've been privileged.

Grade: B

DISCUSSION QUESTIONS
(Child leads discussion.)

1. How well has Dad covered this lesson before?
2. Does Dad practice what he preaches regarding this lesson, or is he a hypocrite?
3. How important do you think college is for your plans?
4. On a scale from one to ten, how much do you agree with this statement? "I need to make my own mistakes and figure things out for myself."
5. What would help you make good decisions "one after another"?

NOTES:

13. ONE BAD RELATIONSHIP

Celebrity: Whitney Houston and Bobby Brown, Singers

Story

Musical legend Whitney Houston married R&B star Bobby Brown in 1992. Twenty years later, divorced and overdosed on cocaine, she was found lying facedown in her own bath water in a Beverly Hills hotel room. How did she go from being one of the greatest recording artists of all time to such a low place?

She did a lot of drugs and married the wrong man.

Whitney Houston was born in 1963 in New Jersey. Her music career didn't take very long to get started. Her mother was a choir minister at the church she grew up in, and Whitney sang with her from the time she was a child through her teen years. She wasn't just talented, though. She was also quickly becoming famous for her beauty. She was one of the first African American women to grace the cover of *Seventeen* magazine. She was signed by Clive Davis of Arista Records after he saw her singing in a nightclub at nineteen years old.

Over the next three years, Houston and Clive worked on her first album. Her debut album, *Whitney Houston*, produced three number-one hits, and it was the number-one album in 1986. From there, she only became more successful. She released her sophomore album, *Whitney*, in 1987. It sold millions of copies across the world and rewarded her with her first Grammy. She was worth tens of millions of dollars. Shortly after the releases of her first two albums, she got married.

Bobby Brown was born in 1969, six years after Houston. He was the victim of gang violence as a child, and he grew up surrounded by poverty. Brown was both shot and stabbed before he was twenty. He did not grow up with a pool in the backyard, nor did he attend a Catholic high school like his future wife did, and he often had to resort to petty theft to scrape by.

Like Houston, Brown sang in a church choir growing up. That was where he realized the scope of his talents. Prior to his marriage to Houston in 1992, he released several albums containing many popular songs, but he was never as popular as Houston. He married a woman who was older and more successful than he was.

Whitney Houston reportedly snorted cocaine on July 18, 1992, the day she married Bobby Brown. That revelation didn't come from some sneaky photographer or gossip hound; rather, it was reported by her new husband. He explained that he knew Houston was a drug user when he married her, but he said, "It only made me love . . . her more."[60] However, Houston wasn't the only one in the relationship who was addicted. Brown also admittedly consumed large amounts of illegal drugs. In fact, if Brown can be believed, he didn't start to consume hardcore drugs until he married Houston. Just like Brown's drug use became worse after the marriage, so did Houston's. According to Houston's former assistant, "It really got bad for her . . . after her marriage to Bobby."[61]

So, both parties involved in the marriage knew that the other was a drug user. Both seemed to feed off one another's addiction, intensifying their own usage. Drugs were one of the focal points of their relationship, period.

Where Houston's career had once been so fantastic, it began to unravel during her marriage. In 2002, Houston was interviewed by Diane Sawyer and admitted to abusing alcohol, marijuana, cocaine, and prescription drugs.[62] However, she claimed she was done with all of it. She made it sound like she had overcome her addiction. Sadly, that was not the case. She entered rehab in 2004 and 2005, and finally divorced Brown in 2007.

Houston's family staged an intervention that same year to force her to enter rehab again. The rest of her career consisted of more canceled shows, more drugs, more rehab, and eventually the overdose that led to her death.

Bobby Brown didn't have much of a career after he married Houston. He only made one more album that no one remembers. He was much more famous for his contentious marriage and being Mr. Whitney Houston. He was arrested several times on drug- and alcohol-related charges. The biggest spike in Brown's post-marriage notoriety came in 2003, when he struck his wife in the face and was arrested for assault.[63] The downward spiral continued with *Being Bobby Brown*, a 2005 reality show depicting the life of Houston and Brown that shed new light on the darkness of their lives and relationship. No one watched the show to see Brown; Houston was the draw. It was shocking to compare the elegant image she presented in the late '80s against the low-rent addict she had become nearly twenty years later. The unpopular show was canceled after one season.

One bright spot existed in the troubled marriage: their daughter, Bobbi Kristina, who was born on March 4, 1993. Obviously, she witnessed her parents' drug habit firsthand. There are accounts of her parents smoking crack and being verbally abusive toward each other, including in their daughter's presence.[64]

The union of Houston and Brown became a melting pot of drug abuse, physical abuse, and sordid irresponsibility. They only intensified each other's substance-abuse problems and ruined their respective careers. Their families became estranged, and Brown reportedly wasn't even welcomed to sit near Houston's family at her funeral on February 12, 2012.[65] Her distraught only child, Bobbi Kristina, was hospitalized twice in the twelve hours after discovering her mother had died.[66]

In a heartbreaking parallel to her mother's tragic end, Bobbi Kristina struggled with drug addiction and unhealthy, controlling relationships. She was found unresponsive in a tub in her Atlanta home on January 31, 2015, and was in a coma for seven months before dying in hospice care at age twenty-two. An autopsy showed she had ingested a fatal cocktail of morphine, cocaine, alcohol, and prescription drugs, but the medical examiner could not determine if her cause of death was an accident, suicide, or homicide.[67] In November 2016, a judge in Atlanta entered an order requiring that Bobbi Kristina Brown's partner, Nick Gordon, pay $36 million in a wrongful death case.[68]

Lesson

Whitney Houston was not blameless, to be sure. She was involved in drugs long before Bobby Brown came along and made things worse. However, we are the company that we keep. With whom we surround ourselves defines not only who we are now, but also who we *will become in the future.*

In 1992, Houston married a drug user who promoted her own drug habit. She married a man who encouraged her personal destruction rather than helping her improve herself—a man who "loved her more" *because of her drug use.* Obviously, Brown has no concept of what love is. He brought out the worst in his spouse. Tragically, by marrying Brown, Houston sealed her fate. His future became her future, and they went down together.

What if Houston hadn't married Brown? Would she still be alive? Would she have had a happy family? Would her successful career have continued? Such questions are the great unknowns of the road not taken.

We need to encourage our daughters to have their own houses in order and to avoid the Bobby Browns of the world. To be fair, our sons need to avoid the Whitney Houstons of the world too. We need to be watchful that our children enter relationships with those who actively bring out their best qualities, not stoke any dark or destructive impulses. That's not to say that any person with a rough past is off limits; just make sure it shaped them into a better person. Above all, marry someone who doesn't make you want to snort cocaine on your wedding day.

• MEGGIE'S TAKE •

I pretty much agree with my dad here. I appreciate his statement near the end about not ruling out people with pasts, because I do think that people can change. I think my big takeaway here is not to be in a relationship with someone who brings out the worst qualities in you. Everyone has negative qualities, and you should be with someone who loves you for who you are (negatives and all), but also pushes you to bring out the best qualities in yourself, not the worst. And don't forget, you need to be that person for them too.

Grade: A-

DISCUSSION QUESTIONS
(Child leads discussion.)

1. How well has Dad covered this lesson before?
2. Does Dad practice what he preaches regarding this lesson, or is he a hypocrite?
3. Which statement do you agree with more?
    a. My partner should love me for who I am.
    b. My partner should push me to be better.
4. Which "worst qualities" in your own life are you watching out for?
5. How do you see your parents bringing out the best (or worst) in each other?

NOTES:

14. ONE NIP (OR TUCK)

Celebrity: Jennifer Grey, Actress

Story

Jennifer Grey was the sweetheart of millions of moviegoers in 1987. *Dirty Dancing*, the movie that also brought Patrick Swayze to fame, had cemented her status as one of America's most beloved young actresses. Bright, talented, and ready to continue an exciting career, there was only one thing she didn't like about looking forward: her nose. To the public, it was her defining feature. Grey's unique nose and overall look, coupled with her acting talent, separated her from other young actresses. She didn't see it that way, and in 1989 Grey got a nose job.

Stop for a minute and try to remember a movie that Jennifer Grey was in after 1989. If you can't think of any, here's a list: *Bloodhounds of Broadway, Wind, Lover's Knot, Portraits of a Killer, Red Meat, Bounce*, and *In Your Eyes*. Do any of those ring a bell? But everybody knows *Dirty Dancing*. What makes that film different? Most of her leading roles were within a decade of *Dirty Dancing*, so it wasn't that she lacked a youthful appearance. Her personality never changed. She was still a talented actor. Many of the movies she was in after 1987 featured stars with reputations as significant as Swayze's. The thing that distinguished the *Dirty Dancing* Jennifer Grey from all those other Jennifer Grey roles was her appearance. She literally looked like a different person.

Like most people who get a nose job, she just wanted a slightly more appealing nose. She wasn't trying to look completely different. Unfortunately, she came out of surgery with a very different face. As she said herself, "I went into the operating room a celebrity and came out anonymous. It was the nose job from hell. I'll always be this once-famous actress nobody recognizes because of a nose job."[69]

The next big moment of her post–*Dirty Dancing* career wouldn't come until 2010, when Grey won *Dancing with the Stars*. Yet the topic of the "nose job from hell" never went away. If you search "bad celebrity plastic surgery," Jennifer Grey is always there at the top of the list. She's the celebrity plastic-surgery cautionary tale. As an actress, she had to stay in the public eye to remain relevant and not fade away. She had to do public appearances and media interviews. Yet her nose job was the elephant in the room for any interview. She couldn't avoid the topic. It was very upsetting for her to know that so many interviews focused at least as much on her past (her *Dirty Dancing* role and her nose job) than showed interest in her future projects.

Jennifer Grey's career took a very serious downturn after her rhinoplasty surgery. Not only was getting a nose job a bad personal decision, as it changed who she was in the eyes of other people, but it was a very bad business decision, as she never got another role like Baby in *Dirty Dancing*. Patrick Swayze's famous line "Nobody puts Baby in the corner" remains iconic, but is off the mark. Rhinoplasty surgery put Jennifer Grey's career in a deep, deep corner.

Lesson

What makes a successful, up-and-coming actress question her appearance to the point of altering it? As Grey alluded to later in life, it was simple insecurity. She didn't have the confidence to accept the unique person she was. Instead of embracing her unique look, she eliminated it in favor of resembling everyone else. She made herself anonymous.

The effects of body image on self-esteem can be especially powerful during the teenage years. Body image is a big problem in our society, and can lead to depression, social anxiety, eating disorders, and surgical interventions.

- According to the Dove Self-Esteem Project, six out of ten girls are so concerned with the way they look that they opt out of important activities.[70]
- The American Society of Plastic and Reconstructive Surgeons finds that more than 236,000 cosmetic procedures were performed on patients ages nineteen and younger in 2012. Some of the most common types of plastic surgery teens choose include nose jobs and corrections of protruding ears, too-large breasts, asymmetrical breasts, and scarring caused by acne or injuries.[71]

Even more distressing is how cosmetic-surgery apps and makeover games are targeting children, making them feel dissatisfied with their own faces and bodies. A report commissioned by the London-based Nuffield Council on Bioethics and published in *The Guardian* on July 22, 2017, identified several games, including "Plastic Surgery Princess" and "Plastic Surgery Simulator," which allow players to alter the image of their own face and body.[72] Others, such as "Dream Cosmetic Surgery," feature an "ugly" princess or "fat" woman who can be made beautiful if she goes under the knife.

"We've been shocked by some of the evidence we've seen, including makeover apps and cosmetic surgery 'games' that target girls as young as nine," said Jeanette Edwards, professor of social anthropology at the University of Manchester, who chaired the council's inquiry. "There is a daily bombardment from advertising and through social-media channels like Facebook, Instagram, and Snapchat that relentlessly promote unrealistic and often discriminatory messages on how people, especially girls and women, 'should' look."

Let's instill a positive self-image in our children at every stage of their development. Should we take care of our bodies and stay fit? Sure. But putting too much emphasis on physical beauty is harmful to our kids' emotional well-being and ultimate happiness as adults. In time, physical looks begin to fade as a normal part of aging. As dads, we need to model this truth and tell our sons and daughters to value beauty on the inside above physical attributes. They must resist peer pressure to transform themselves into someone else's vision of attractiveness.

• MEGGIE'S TAKE •

Body image is a huge problem, and I personally know tons of people affected by it, including myself. Unfortunately, as much as you tell your kids to focus on "beauty on the inside," that's not going to stop them from constantly comparing themselves to their friends, acquaintances, celebrities, and random people on the street. I think one of the biggest pitfalls parents fall into here is saying all the right things but doing all the wrong ones. Kids are going to hear the "inner beauty" argument everywhere. In fact, it's so common that it will probably become almost meaningless to your kid. What will become meaningful are the much subtler (and seemingly innocuous) things you do.

Here's an example. Your teenager comes home from summer camp or college and you say, "Did you lose a couple of pounds? You look good!" You're giving them a compliment, right? But here's what your kid probably hears: "Yeah, you didn't look so good this spring. This is better. Whatever you've been doing differently, keep up the good work!" God forbid, if your kid used extreme measures to lose those couple of pounds, this will validate their choice to do so, and even (unintentionally) encourage them to keep up potentially destructive behaviors.

Here's another example. You're opening the mail and get a Christmas card from an old college friend. "Wow, Jill really let herself go!" you say. Now, this comment has nothing to do with your kid, so it shouldn't be a problem, right? Wrong. Here's what your kid gets from this comment: If I am ever the same size as this person, people will think I'm disgusting. If I gain weight and people see a picture, they will make a comment about my weight. This person is ugly, and if I look like her then I am too.

It's annoying how subtle this stuff is, right? I think the only answer here is to stop judging other people (which is way easier said than done). We have no idea what is going on in other people's lives. There's tons of reasons why people gain weight or look a certain way, many of which they have literally no control over. If you can't stop judging, then at least keep it to yourself.

Why do you think Jennifer Grey felt so insecure about her nose? Even if no one ever made a negative comment to her (which is extremely unlikely), she still felt bad about it because our society values certain features over others. You can't do anything about society, but you can make sure you don't contribute to the negativity your kid is going to encounter in it.

Grade: B-

DISCUSSION QUESTIONS
(Child leads discussion.)

1. How well has Dad covered this lesson before?
2. Does Dad practice what he preaches regarding this lesson, or is he a hypocrite?
3. What does the term "inner beauty" mean to you?
4. What would it take for you to stop comparing yourself to other people?
5. What's the first step you can take to stop judging other people?

NOTES:

15. ONE SEXT

Celebrity: Anthony Weiner, US Congressman

Story

New York Congressman Anthony Weiner tweeted a picture of his crotch on May 27, 2011. That's right, a man named *Weiner* tweeted—from his personal account—a lewd picture of his privates. He did this while he was a sitting US congressman. Then, as we are accustomed to politicians doing, he tried to cover it up.

Up until then, Weiner had a promising career. At age twenty-seven, he was the youngest New York City council member ever elected. Seven years later, he won a close election to replace Charles Schumer as a member of the US House of Representatives. Between 1998 and 2011, Weiner served six terms in Congress and made a failed attempt to become the mayor of New York City.

It was May 2011 when things started to heat up for the married congressman. The tweet that started it all was sent on the night of May 27. A picture of a man wearing underwear that left very little to the imagination was posted online for about four minutes before being deleted. It wasn't immediately clear whether the photograph was taken of or by Weiner, but the possibility that a congressman had just posted a lewd picture publicly for thousands of people to see was about to make the media rounds.

Throughout the next several days, Weiner stuck to saying that his Twitter account had been hacked and called the matter "a prank—not a terribly creative one."[73] Then Weiner got a lawyer. On May 31, Weiner held a press conference in which he refused to answer direct questions about the Twitter incident. Earlier that same day, Andrew Breitbart was on CNN laying out the facts of the matter for an international audience and calling for an FBI investigation. The pressure was on for Weiner.

Then things got a bit ridiculous. In an interview with MSNBC, Weiner replied, "I can't say with certitude" when asked whether the picture his account tweeted was of him.[74] Think about that for a second. A United States congressman said he wasn't sure whether a picture that distinctly featured outlined male genitalia inside a particular pair of underwear taken in a particular room was of him. We tend to think if it weren't him in the picture, Weiner would deny it with complete "certitude," since presumably he was aware of his own anatomy, his own underwear, and what rooms he was in where he didn't permit such photographs. The non-denial denial was preposterous, and only served to fuel the media fire.

"Weinergate," as the scandal became known, only intensified. On June 6, a woman came forward to reveal that she had been engaged in sexual communications with Congressman Weiner. The news networks covered the unfolding stories of multiple women across the country revealing their explicit messages, phone calls, and conversations with Weiner. The day culminated at a press event in which the congressman admitted to sending the obscene picture on his personal Twitter account.

Despite pressure from many sources, Weiner refused to resign from his position. The next ten days were a whirlwind of explicit pictures of Weiner being leaked from various sources. High-ranking members of Weiner's party called on him to resign, including President Barack Obama. That may have been the final nail in the coffin of public opinion for Weiner. He resigned from Congress on June 16, 2011. It appeared his political life was over.

Not so fast.

In May of 2013, Weiner announced his second mayoral campaign in New York City. About one month later, the public learned he had been having more online sexual conversations with women throughout 2012, *after* his public humiliation and resignation. These sexual conversations were, just like the 2011 scandals, published in graphic detail for all to see.

Weiner lost the election and has not held office since. Just after losing the mayoral election, he gave this quote: "I'm fifty years old, and I need to find a new career."[75]

Lesson

Don't take sexually explicit photos of yourself, and don't let anybody else take them! Is that so difficult? If your body isn't available to be circulated on social media, television news, and the internet in general, it won't be circulated. Simple! And if someone does take lewd pictures of you without your knowledge or consent, then get a lawyer, pronto.

Dads, our teenagers have Snapchat. This means that they can send *self-deleting* pictures, messages, and videos to others at any time. At least, some teenagers think the inappropriate and compromising pictures are self-deleting and therefore can't be saved and then broadcast forever on the internet.

Not so.

The problem, of course, is that they are deceiving themselves, because anyone can take a screenshot of a Snapchat before it deletes, and then post it to the world on Facebook, Twitter, or any other social-media platform. Once it's out there, it can never be retrieved. It is there for all of posterity. Forever.

Scary Statistics

Pornography is a huge battlefield for youth culture, and pornography is winning. Big time. The race isn't close. Consider these statistics:

- 43 percent of people start viewing porn between the ages of eleven and thirteen.[76]
- 32 percent of teens admit to intentionally accessing nude or pornographic content online. Of these, 43 percent do so on a weekly basis.

Only 12 percent of parents know their teens are accessing pornography.[77]
- 70 percent of teens aged fifteen through seventeen say they have accidentally stumbled across pornography online.[78]
- 71 percent of teens have done something to hide what they do online from their parents (including clearing browser history, minimizing a browser when in view, deleting inappropriate videos, lying about behavior, using a phone instead of a computer, blocking parents with social-media privacy settings, using private browsing, disabling parental controls, or having email or social-media accounts unknown to parents).[79]
- 56 percent of divorces involve one party having "an obsessive interest in pornographic websites."[80]
- There is a 22 percent increase in risk of committing sexual offenses for those who view pornographic material.[81]

Sadly, pornography seems to have a similar level of use among those who have religious objections to it as it does among those who don't.

- 64 percent of self-identified Christian men and 15 percent of self-identified Christian women view pornography at least once a month (compared to 65 percent of non-Christian men and 30 percent of non-Christian women).[82]
- 37 percent of Christian men and 7 percent of Christian women view pornography at least several times a week (compared to 42 percent of non-Christian men and 11 percent of non-Christian women).[83]

Lesson

Pornography is complex and encompasses wide-ranging forms of entertainment. It exists in movies, music, books, and the internet. Pornography is embedded in our culture. How, then, can we ensure that what goes into the minds of our children, young adults, and ourselves is not harmful?

Caution isn't enough. Proactivity, education, and communication are the only hopes to mount an effective fight. Passivity and silence result in defeat.

It goes without saying that when we put bad things into our bodies, such as tobacco, illegal drugs, excessive alcohol, or excessive sugar, we do harm to our bodies. If we see one hundred sexual acts in half an hour, how will that affect our minds? Our marriages? How we treat the opposite sex? More importantly, how would that affect the *forming mind* of a teenager? There isn't one precise answer, but research does point to porn exposure having the potential to change the pathways of the brain.

Pornography is the mental equivalent of the worst diet you could think of. Unfortunately, the effects of pornography aren't as easily reversible as the effects of too much sugar. Diet, exercise, and medicine can change the shape of the body in a relatively predictable manner. There is no such predictive scientific formula for reversing the negative psychological effects of pornography. Pornography addiction is unique in that one does not need to spend any money or leave the comfort of home to become addicted. Just access the internet. It only takes one click and eleven letters to search "violent porn." The hassle factor for pornography access is uncomfortably low.

As fathers, we must confront the reality that pornography is easy to access and easy to hide. This epidemic requires a meaningful dialogue with the younger generation to keep bad habits from forming. Guaranteed, talking to our kids about pornography will not be a comfortable conversation, but it needs to happen nonetheless. In addition, as adults, we need to get our own internet-consumption house in order, lest we become the hypocrites that teenagers can so easily spot.

Though dialogue with our kids about the dangers of pornography is important, we can't stop there. Action is required. This includes not viewing movies that are basically pornography disguised as a storyline. Such movies are commonplace under the auspices of "R" or "NC-17" ratings. Many R-rated movies contain lewd scenes that exist in other forms of online porn, and yet they are still watched without concern by teenagers (and even families!). The movie industry has given its seal of approval to movies with pornographic content, but that does not mean that we should. If I'm watching a movie with my kid (or grandparent) and we're both uncomfortable viewing certain scenes together, should either one of us be watching it?

There's a distinction to be made here between the different types of R ratings. Watching movies like *Saving Private Ryan* and *Braveheart* isn't a problem—there is historical value in these films, and no one feels uncomfortable. On the other hand, try watching *Fifty Shades of Grey* with your kids and grandma—awkward!

The upshot: Pornography is damaging, and there are clear correlations between pornography abuse and sexual violence, relationship damage, and poor mental health. Pornography's damaging effects can only be stopped by refusing to consume it. From a young age, we must instill a sense of honor, self-respect, and self-discipline among our children, or the internet will do the opposite.

As fathers, we need to attack this problem head-on. Let's talk with our teenagers about the risks of sexting and use Congressman Weiner as a cautionary tale. After the awkward pornography talk, how bad can the sexting conversation be?

Epilogue

Unfortunately, Representative Weiner did not learn his lesson after his career-ending sexting mistakes of 2011, 2012, and 2013. In 2016, it was revealed that Weiner sexted with other women during 2015. He even exchanged lewd online messages with an underaged girl, which transformed him from a dirtbag pervert to a full-fledged sex offender. His long-suffering wife, Huma Abedin, finally had enough and announced their separation in the summer of 2016. She filed for divorce in June 2017, five days after his sentencing for his online exchanges with a minor. He is serving a twenty-one-month sentence in federal prison in Massachusetts.[84] Not only did sexting ruin Weiner's career, but it also ruined his marriage, reputation, and freedom.

• MEGGIE'S TAKE •

Yikes, that's embarrassing. As with all potentially risky behaviors, this is a cost-benefit game. If the benefit of sexting outweighs the potential costs of your pictures being leaked, used for revenge by a jealous ex, or other unfortunate things, go for it. Just don't be surprised if you get publicly humiliated. And please, for the love of God, do not post any of your pictures *publicly on social media*. If you're going to be dumb while you're doing something risky, don't even bother.

Grade: A–

DISCUSSION QUESTIONS
(Child leads discussion.)

1. How well has Dad covered this lesson before?
2. Does Dad practice what he preaches regarding this lesson, or is he a hypocrite?
3. How likely do you think it is that anyone in your life would use a picture against you?
4. Do you think sexting is dangerous if you're in a committed relationship?
5. What would you do if someone sent you explicit photos?

NOTES:

• CHAPTER 3 •

THE CHILDHOOD DUMB DECISIONS

In this final series of decisions, the good news is that our children aren't dead and they are still on the road to a solid future. These decisions do no lasting damage, but leave us dads wondering, "What were they thinking?"

16. ONE TATTOO

Celebrity: Johnny Depp, Actor

Story

Johnny Depp is an international movie star known best for his role as Jack Sparrow in the Pirates of the Caribbean movies. Winona Rider is a two-time Academy Award–nominated actress. In 1990, they both starred in the successful movie *Edward Scissorhands*. A Hollywood romance blossomed and an engagement followed, with Winona sporting a dazzling engagement ring. Johnny's devotion then took a more permanent turn— he inked his right bicep with a tattoo that read "Winona Forever." As it turned out, forever was just twenty-four months! Predictably, the ink outlasted the Beverly Hills romance. As for Winona, she slipped the ring off her finger and moved on. For Johnny, he had a more permanent reminder—and a problem. For many reasons, including being the butt of many late-night comedian jokes, Johnny had the tattoo altered to read "Wino Forever." Perhaps Johnny has gotten it right.

Or, maybe Johnny was just getting started. Fast-forward twenty years, and Johnny was at it again. Actress Amber Heard was his then-girlfriend and soon-to-be wife. Depp had "Slim," Heard's nickname, tattooed on his right knuckles. They were married February 3, 2015, with the "Slim" tattoo going strong—at least for fifteen months. Heard filed for divorce on May 23, 2016. With the relationship over, he again had to remove a romance tattoo. Oh, Johnny, not again. This time he changed "Slim" to "Scum," the classless point being impossible to miss.

Tattoos are a young person's game. But among the young, tattoos are no longer for the edgy outliers; they have gone mainstream, even suburban.

- 36 percent of Americans between the ages of eighteen and twenty-five have at least one tattoo.[85]
- 40 percent of Americans between the ages of twenty-six to forty sport a tattoo.[86]
- A 2006 study from the *Journal of American Academy of Dermatology* found that 24 percent of Americans between ages eighteen and fifty are tattooed.[87]
- 50 percent of Americans who get a tattoo eventually want to remove it, according to the American Society of Dermatology Surgery.[88]

Sporting a tattoo just doesn't move the rebel meter like it used to. It's hard to prove you are not like the other 99 percent of your peers. Now, nearly 40 percent of your classmates have a tattoo just like you. By the time our kids graduate, they will have more classmates *with* tattoos than without tattoos. In a cruel twist of fate, classmates without tattoos will be fewer in number and thereby more distinctive than the tattoo-wearing *majority*.

How cruel to the rebel class.

If having a tattoo fails to make you stand out, then play your trump card: Have your tattoo removed. Sure, it is expensive and painful, but now you are in the most unique group of all: the I-had-my-tattoo-removed club! Let your classmates try to match that.

But wait. News flash: Tattoo removals are yesterday's news. Magician Criss Angel, star of A&E's *Mindfreak*, had stitches of his initials put in his skin—an A inside a backward C—and then had the stitches removed to form a scar. So forget tattoos or tattoo removals, the "in" thing now is intentional skin mutilation by way of unnecessary medical stitches followed by their removal to form a scar. Think ahead and consider scar-revision surgery to remove an unnecessary scar in the first place. Then, when one of your classmates is sporting a tattoo, tattoo removal, or scar, you can one-up them by showing them the outcome of your scar-revision surgery.

Lesson

Maybe we can convince our children that they are already unique individuals who don't need to prove it with tattoos, tattoo removals, scars, scar revisions, body piercings, or hair dye. No, probably not. But if they must ink themselves, try "Daddy Forever." That has a nice ring to it.

• MEGGIE'S TAKE •

Okay, Dad, really? What did tattoos ever do to you? News flash: Not everyone is getting tattoos to "stand out." Getting a tattoo isn't some power play that we're all making to prove we're different from everyone else. We are fully aware that a lot of people our age have tattoos. Sure, there are probably some people who are trying to stand out from the crowd by getting a tattoo, but other people want one in order to fit in. Still others want a tattoo because it means something personal and meaningful to them. Believe it or not, some people even get a tattoo in a place only they can see, and don't even tell anyone else about it! Crazy, right?

Here's another crazy thought: It's really none of your concern. Would you comment if a person wore clothes you didn't happen to think were stylish? Would you have a problem if they pierced their ears and wore huge earrings every day? I'm thinking not.

So, why care how a person looks? Some people might regret their tattoo. We all have regrets. But remember, it's not your problem. The message and use of tattoos are changing. They are becoming mainstream. Better hop on board.

Grade: F

Dad's response to Meggie's Take: Meggie has a tattoo.

DISCUSSION QUESTIONS
(Child leads discussion.)

1. How well has Dad covered this lesson before?
2. Does Dad practice what he preaches regarding this lesson, or is he a hypocrite?
3. What is your family's policy on tattoos?
4. Do you agree with your parents on that policy?
5. Would you ever get a tattoo? Why or why not?

NOTES:

17. ONE CELEBRITY INSIGHT, COURTESY OF GEORGE CLOONEY

With the exception of John Krasinski, the celebrities profiled have taken their lumps, and for good reasons. But to be fair, there are many celebrities who appreciate the gravity of fatherhood and have thoughtful advice worth sharing. Enter actor George Clooney.

In 2006, George Clooney was named *People* magazine's "Sexiest Man Alive." That's pretty sexy, considering there are more than three billion men in the world. He is at the top of the celebrity mountain. In his 2006 interview, on the topic of kids, Clooney told *People*, "I think it's the biggest responsibility you'll ever have, and it's not something to be taken lightly. I don't have that thing in me that says, 'must do it.' I don't see myself ever having kids."[89]

Finally! Some solid parenting advice from Hollywood. Clooney is right; fatherhood is a huge responsibility, and it shouldn't be taken lightly. If the dad "thing" is not in you, then don't be one. *Stay childless.*

Epilogue

Never mind.

It turns out Clooney's destiny would involve the joy of changing diapers and midnight bottle feedings, after all. Three years after his celebrated marriage to British human-rights attorney Amal Alamuddin, the couple welcomed twins, Alexander and Ella. "Suddenly, you're responsible for other people, which is terrifying," the first-time father told the Associated Press after the June 6, 2017, birth of his children.[90]

In a September 14, 2017, interview with the *Daily Mail*, Clooney confessed, "Look, I'm fifty-six years old and I didn't think it was going to happen for me. I thought my life would be focused on my career, not relationships, and I'd sort of accepted that. Then I met Amal and I thought, 'Well, I have this incredible relationship, this is wonderful.' And then, all of a sudden we have these two knuckleheads around who make me laugh every day."[91]

Clooney's happy ending with his new family offers another lesson to young people: Wait until you're ready to embark on the awesome responsibility and adventure of parenthood.

• CHAPTER 4 •

THE RECONCILING DAD: HORIZONTAL RECONCILIATION (CHILD-TO-PARENT)

<u>Horizontal Reconciliation</u>
Parent ⟶ Child

Horizontal reconciliation is a prerequisite for being an effective messenger. There is such a thing as vertical reconciliation, but we'll hold that for the next chapter. Horizontal reconciliation means being in right relationships with our fellow man so that our message—secular or spiritual—will be heard and considered. If we are in broken relationships with others, we are lousy messengers with no relational capital, and our message will be ignored. In the parental context, horizontal reconciliation means we have a solid relationship with our children—namely, we are in a reconciled, not divisive, parental-child state. By consistently being a reconciling parent, we have a chance that our message will be heard, considered, and maybe even nudge our children toward a stable and productive life. By consistently being a divisive dad, we're voiceless.

Are we reconciled with our children, making us effective messengers?

We should already be on our way. Hopefully, we spent some quality time together sharing edgy celebrity stories. That couldn't hurt. But more is required from us to accomplish true horizontal reconciliation with our children, making us effective messengers.

The rest of Part I is a practical guide to become Reconciling Dads by filling four buckets with ten deposits. Will our efforts succeed? Maybe, maybe not.

To illustrate the great challenge of investing in our children, we employ a simple metaphor: the *family checking account*. Many of us think that fatherhood is about being a good provider. That is certainly a part of it. Along with our spouse, we need to take care of the needs (and wants) of our families. Food, shelter, water, energy, transportation, team uniforms, ballet lessons, smartphones, video-gaming, cable TV, and all the rest are to be paid from the *family checking account*. We are very careful with our family checking accounts. We make sure the account has sufficient funds so we can provide for our families and validate our role as good providers.

Meet Mr. Banker. He is the boss of our family checking accounts. Mr. Banker is very strict with us dads. He monitors the accounts. He keeps track of our deposits and withdrawals. If we withdraw more than we deposit, then we are out of balance and our checks bounce. That makes Mr. Banker very unhappy, and he punishes us with fees for "insufficient funds." The fees cause even less money to be available, leading us into a bad, dysfunctional cycle. If we don't get back into balance, Mr. Banker may even close our accounts entirely. It is never good to be overdrawn with Mr. Banker.

Yet, Mr. Banker is a pushover when compared to Mr. Kid.

The Dad/Child Checking Account

On the day they were born, our children automatically opened a *dad/child checking account*. This is a different kind of checking account. This time we're not dealing with Mr. Banker, but instead with Mr. Kid. Mr. Kid is the boss of the dad/child checking account, and he's very strict with us dads. He monitors the account. He keeps track of the deposits and withdrawals of the dad checking account. If we withdraw more than we deposit, then we are out of balance, and that makes Mr. Kid very unhappy. He will punish us in a variety of ways, and we can easily find ourselves in a bad, dysfunctional dad/child cycle. If we don't get back into balance soon, Mr. Kid may even freeze our account, or at least put it on a temporary hold. It is never good to be overdrawn with Mr. Kid. As dads, the ultimate failure is if a child declares our dad/child checking account to be bankrupt and closes our relational account.

To many of us, running a negative bank balance would be embarrassing, and bouncing a check downright shameful. The recipient of the bad check thinks (rightfully) we're deadbeats. He may tell others. Not making timely payments is disclosed to the credit-reporting agencies (Equifax, Transunion, Experian), our credit scores take a hit, and retailers we deal with know about it when looking at our electronic credit file. We may even be at the checkout counter one day and our credit cards get rejected. Oh, the shame of it all. Such an outcome is nothing less than an affront to our good name, something to be avoided at all costs.

Yet while many of us wouldn't dream of bouncing a check, we don't feel the same embarrassment in running negative or low balances in our dad/child checking account. Frankly, many of us don't know what our balances are. It's hard to know. We get no monthly statements from our children like we do from Mr. Banker. Sure, we've invested time, effort, and energy into them, but is it enough? Are these things even knowable?

Actually, we dads are quite successful at convincing ourselves that we have done an "excellent" or "very good" job at being fathers. The statistics show how fully we have deceived ourselves. The first step in being a Reconciling Dad is to stop our own self-deception.

18. SELF-DECEPTION MUST STOP

A lot of us think we're millionaire dads, yet our dad/child balances are near zero. Being a dad isn't easy, and we're all for giving ourselves the benefit of the doubt, but it is amazing how good we think we are compared with the work we are putting in. Many of us are handing in C+ work but think we're on the Dad Dean's List. It is insane. None of us went to Dad School before siring a child. So, where does such confidence come from?

The Pew Research Center provides the following insights:

Among all parents with children under age eighteen, 24 percent say they have done an excellent job, and an additional 45 percent say they have done a very good job. Some 24 percent say they have done a good job, and only 6 percent rate their job as parents as fair or poor.[92]

Let's summarize:

- 69 percent of all parents report they have done an "excellent" or "very good job."
- 93 percent of all parents report they have done an "excellent," "very good," or "good" job.

So, nearly seven out of ten parents graded themselves as having done a "very good" job or better. And more than nine out of ten did at least a "good" job or better? Wow. This appears to be terrific news. With 70 percent of us doing a "very good" job or better, we must be incredibly dedicated parents who really put in the time and energy to produce well-adjusted, productive offspring.

Of course, the obvious problem is that none of us can be objective about our own parental performance.

We can't all be in the ninety-third percentile! Asking a dad about his paternal performance is no way to accurately measure such performance. Simply put, we are very good at deceiving ourselves.

Reality Check: The One-Hour-a-Day Dad

Let's compare how we graded ourselves against the work we actually put in. According to the Pew Research Center, in 1960 the average father spent a paltry 2.5 hours per week on childcare activities. Fifty years later in 2011, that number increased to 7 hours per week. Yes, that is per week, not per day.

So in 2011, before everyone had a smartphone, we spent seven hours per week (up from an incredibly low two and half hours per week in 1965), or *one hour per day*, on being a father? Remarkably, again according to the Pew Research Center, 57 percent of fathers said being a father was "extremely important" to their identity. It may be "extremely important" to our identities, but it is not at all important to our schedules. The big finish: Approximately 69 percent of parents believe they have done an "excellent" or "very good" job by spending *one hour per day with their children*? Either parenting simply doesn't require much time to be "very good," or we are suffering from serious self-deception about what it takes to be very good fathers.

One hour per day is a wake-up call. Will more time invested ensure our children become better citizens? No. But how does one hour from us compare against the hours and hours our children spend with their peer group each day?

So, how can we be Reconciling Dads to our children? How can we have a positive dad/child checking-account balance in the eyes of our children? The same way all positive account balances happen: We must make deposits—lots of them—and avoid making too many withdrawals.

19. THE FOUR SECULAR BUCKETS AND TEN DEPOSITS TO BE RECONCILING DADS

FILLING THE BUCKETS

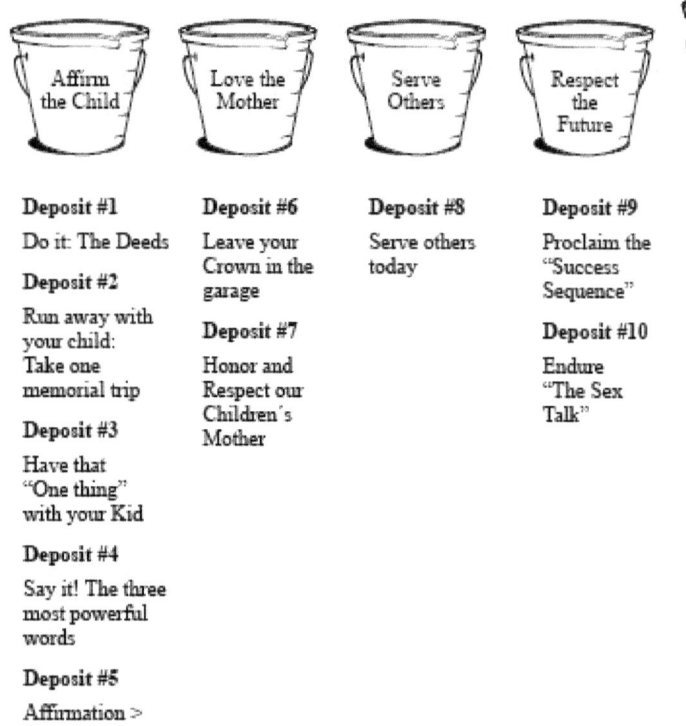

Deposit #1
Do it: The Deeds

Deposit #2
Run away with your child: Take one memorial trip

Deposit #3
Have that "One thing" with your Kid

Deposit #4
Say it! The three most powerful words

Deposit #5
Affirmation > Correction

Deposit #6
Leave your Crown in the garage

Deposit #7
Honor and Respect our Children's Mother

Deposit #8
Serve others today

Deposit #9
Proclaim the "Success Sequence"

Deposit #10
Endure "The Sex Talk"

Deposit #11
Believe and point to the Forever Father

We can endeavor to be Reconciling Dads by filling four buckets with ten deposits listed below. (Spoiler alert: There is a life-changing fifth bucket, but that is a spiritual bucket for Part II readers only.) Will these ten deposits help us *reconcile with our children*, nudging them toward stable and productive lives? Maybe, maybe not, but by doing so we satisfy the parental Hippocratic oath: (1) Be humble, and (2) do no harm.

Affirm the Child (Bucket #1)

Deposit #1.	Do It: The Deeds
Deposit #2.	Run Away with Your Child: Take One Memorable Trip Alone
Deposit #3.	Have That "One Thing" with Your Kid
Deposit #4.	Say It! The Three Most Powerful Words
Deposit #5.	Affirmation > Correction 10:1 Ratio

Love the Mother (Bucket #2)

Deposit #6.	Leave Your Crown in the Garage
Deposit #7.	Honor and Respect Your Children's Mother

Serve Others (Bucket #3)

Deposit #8.	Serve Others Today

Respect the Future (Bucket #4)

Deposit #9.	Proclaim the "Success Sequence"
Deposit #10.	Endure "The Sex Talk"

Worship the King (Bucket #5) (For Part II Readers Only)

Deposit #11.	Believe in and Follow the Forever Father

Let's unpack the first four buckets and ten deposits.

20. AFFIRM THE CHILD (BUCKET #1)

BUCKET FILLING

Deposit #1	Do it: The Deeds
Deposit #2	Run away with your child: Take one memorial trip
Deposit #3	Have that "One thing" with your Kid
Deposit #4	Say it! The three most powerful words
Deposit #5	Affirmation > Correction 10:1 Ratio

    To affirm means to give our children appropriate, positive encouragement—an "attaboy" or "bravo" to foster their positive development in three important ways: First, to reinforce a positive value or behavior so it becomes a habit, a way of life; second, when we express a positive opinion of our children, they are more likely to adopt the same opinion of themselves; and third, it is FUN. Our children do something right for the right reason, and we get to point it out to them. That sounds like fun! Mission accomplished!

    Now before we go on, time for a disclaimer. To affirm should not be confused with giving false praise or enabling. Enabling happens when parents do for children what they should do for themselves, delaying growth and maturity.

For example, say there are two friends, Diligent Dennis and Slacker Steve, in the same high school history class, and they enjoy playing video games after school together. A big history paper is coming due. Dennis tells Steve he can't play video games for the next two days so he can work on the history paper. Dennis does the research, writes the paper, and turns it in. On the other hand, Steve keeps playing video games but stops just long enough to crank out a sloppy paper. Then Steve's dad reads the paper, "reworks" it, and Steve turns it in. Both papers receive a B+ grade.

It's easy to see who affirmed and who enabled.

Dennis' dad is the affirmer. He proclaimed, "Bravo," to Dennis on three fronts:

Bravo #1: To Dennis for his time management
Bravo #2: To Dennis for doing the hard work on his own
Bravo #3: ToCed Dennis for getting a good grade

Notice the grade affirmation came last. Dennis' dad knows that by affirming a winning process, the outcome will usually (but not always) take care of itself and repeat itself. And what will Dennis' response be to his dad for (1) paying attention and knowing about the big history paper, and (2) giving three "bravos" concerning the paper? A positive relational moment, to be sure. Will Dennis continue to work hard for himself and his dad's affirmation? Probably. What child does not want their dad's attention and approval? A virtuous cycle created.

Receiving dad's approval is good, but affirmation works best when it changes how our children see themselves. In his best-selling book *The Maxwell Daily Reader*, John Maxwell, citing Dr. J. Sterling Livingston, offers this wise counsel: "People perform consistently as they perceive you expect them to perform."[93] If our children think that we think they are responsible, hardworking people, they are more likely to live up to that positive expectation.

Back to our example. What if Dennis got a D on his history paper? The good news is that the first two "bravos" still apply to cushion the blow. No one said this was easy. Life will throw in some Ds along the way. Importantly, as explained in *The Maxwell Daily Reader*, if a person thinks another has a "high opinion"[94] of him, then he will try to live up to that high expectation. Therefore, regardless of the grade, if Dennis thinks his dad holds a "high opinion" of him, Dennis more likely will hold a "high opinion" *of himself* and will work toward performing in a manner consistent with that high opinion.

What about Slacker Steve? Well, his dad will be "reworking" his papers for a while and probably be writing his college application essay too. Steve does not have a high opinion of himself because his dad has reinforced a negative expectation by having to redo his work. Unfortunately, this type of enabling happens all too often to a child's long-term detriment. Sometimes there is a reckoning when the kid hits the real world. Other times the child skates through. No one said life is fair.

Affirming means giving our children what they need, not what they want, so that they can grow and mature and accomplish the "adulting" process. Affirming helps; enabling hurts. Let's start filling Bucket #1 (Affirm the Child) with five deposits.

21. DO IT: THE DEEDS (DEPOSIT #1)

Doing fun, positive deeds that affirm our children is the most important category of deposits we can make as Disappearing Dads. Our children closely scrutinize our deeds. They will do what we do and discount what we say. Even worse, when our deeds don't match our words, our children instantly sniff out the hypocrisy and hold it against us. Without consistent deeds, withdrawals are out of control, and before long the dad/child checking account is hopelessly overdrawn. To avoid relational bankruptcy, we need to get busy making deposits by doing fun, positive deeds.

This deeds chapter is broken down into subsections: structured and unstructured time. The common denominator and combined power of both is simple: TIME! Time, translated into kid language, means LOVE. Most often, but admittedly not always, there is a straight line in a father-and-child joy equation that goes like this: more time = more deeds = love.

How much time are we talking about exactly? Realistically, what is the minimum number of hours we have to put in to achieve the goal of dad/child relational joy?

The 10,000 Hours Rule to Achieve Excellence

In his bestselling book *Outliers: The Story of Success*, Malcolm Gladwell explains that it takes ten thousand hours to achieve expertise in a particular endeavor. As he puts it:

> The idea that excellence at performing a complex task requires a critical minimum level of practice surfaces again and again in studies of expertise. In fact, researchers have settled on what they believe is the magic number for true expertise: ten thousand hours.[95]

Gladwell illustrates his point with the following examples: Mozart (music), Bobby Fischer (chess), Bill Gates (computers), and the Beatles (music). It's hard to argue with that roster of excellence. Now let's apply Gladwell's principle to fatherhood.

Fatherhood no doubt qualifies as a "complex task," so according to Gladwell, all we need to do is practice being a father for ten thousand hours and we'll be experts. Practice makes perfect (or at least expert), and by achieving expertise we can reach the mountaintop of father/child relational joy. This could be very challenging for those with only one child or just one set of twins, but for the rest of us, maybe we can get there. And even if we don't get there with our oldest children, we'll certainly make the ten-thousand-hour practice mark for our later children. They will be the beneficiaries of our collective fatherly "expertise" from all those hours logged *practicing* on older siblings. Good for the young ones. The time mark of ten thousand hours of fatherly practice seems achievable, but let's run the numbers.

The Pew Research Center Data Revisited

Earlier, we cited a Pew Research Center study that said in 2011 fathers spent seven hours per week, or one hour per day, on being a father. For a moment, let's assume the research is right. In our child's eighteen years, will we meet the ten-thousand-hour mark to be expert fathers?

7 hours per week x 52 weeks per year = 364 hours per year

364 hours per year x 18 years = 6,552 hours

Uh-oh! By this math, we're 3,448 hours, or 35 percent, short of the goal. We're a long way away from being expert dads. At this rate, we would need three children before we logged enough practice hours to be considered experts.

Let's Just Stay Ahead of the Culture

We're not expert dads, according to Gladwell's standard, but maybe we're looking at this the wrong way. It's not the hours logged but the impact accomplished that matters. Social scientists use the term "dose effect" to explain the phenomena that the longer the treatment (or intervention), the more likely the damage done. So, the longer our children are influenced by the culture, the more damage done. To beat the cultural dose effect, we just need to put in more time than the culture to win the influencing game.

Let's see how our time sheet compares to the culture's in the typical day of a teenager:

- Sleep: 8 hours
- School: 8 hours
- Activities: 2 hours
- TV/Media/Technology Use: 3 hours
- Other: 3 hours

Father time fits into the "Other" category, which translates to a maximum of three hours per day. Using the more realistic estimate of two hours per day (which is probably generous), this means we spend 8 percent (2 hours/24 total hours) of a typical day with our children. Taking out sleep, we can bump our total to 12.5 percent (2 hours/16 waking hours) of a typical day. The culture gets the rest.

In terms of time, we are way behind the culture in influencing our children. So, how do we turn that around, putting the culture in the weaker-influencer role?

Unstructured Time to the Rescue

So far, nothing but bad news. We aren't ten-thousand-hour dads, and we spend far less intentional time with our kids than they do with the culture. Is there a way to catch up and sneak in some additional, effective time? Fortunately for us, unstructured time comes to the rescue—but it comes with a price.

If we're going to have unstructured time with our kids, then our golf game and hobbies will suffer. The power of spending time with our kids—structured or unstructured—is not to get to the ten-thousand-hour parental promised land, but to show our kids that spending time with them is more important than spending time away from them, be it on the golf course or at the office. A key side benefit is any time with them means the more time they are away from the culture—a definite twofer. To make this doable, let's even adopt a very loose definition of unstructured time. It can include jumping in on whatever your kids are doing or shooting a quick round of hoops on the driveway. Does TV-watching count? Sure, provided we're watching together and there is some conversation along the way. The key is choosing to be around and be present, to show them that they are the priority even if we're just passing the time together.

Spending unstructured time can present some unexpected opportunities that would otherwise be forever lost. The following is a story about how unstructured time created unexpected memories between father and son.

During a rainy family vacation, the ladies went shopping while the father and his ten-year-old son turned the condo into a "man cave" and passed the afternoon watching TV. Between the dad's work and the son's school, they literally never watched TV together on weekday afternoons. As the dad multitasked between dozing off, perusing a magazine, and flipping channels, he came upon a Rocky marathon, from *Rocky* to *Rocky V*. He looked up and asked, "Do you want to want to watch *Rocky II*?"

His son replied, "No, thanks." The father nodded and returned to sleepily skimming his magazine when his son added, "That's the movie about the football player, right?"

The dad bolted upright as if dunked in ice water, dropped the remote, chucked the magazine against the wall, and in wide-eyed shock asked his son, "You think Rocky Balboa is a football player?"

"Isn't he?" his son calmly replied.

With his head about to explode, the dad was left wondering just how it could be that his ten-year-old son didn't know who Rocky Balboa was. Didn't the schools teach that anymore? Oh, the father failure. Oh, the father shame.

Well, after six hours glued to the TV, both father and son could rest easy. The son had earned his PhD in all things Italian Stallion, his Rocky education complete. The ten-year-old even knew that true Rocky aficionados reject any Rocky movie after *Rocky IV* as an illegitimate and shameless over-commercialization of the true Rocky ideals. And the best part of it all: No one was ever the wiser. As far as the world knew, the time-honored stories of Rocky Balboa had been dutifully passed down from father to son. No child embarrassment, no father shame.

Movies, books, songs, sports teams, and TV shows all compose a bright (or dim) mosaic of the shared father-child experience. A father and child either have special movies, books, songs, sports teams, or TV shows that enrich and intertwine their lives together, or they don't—and are the poorer for it. Rocky may be a fictional character from long ago, but the memory of hours of Rocky movies between father and son on a rainy beach day are very real and fondly remembered. That is the magic of unstructured time.

Most of the time, unstructured time leads to nothing. Yet, on occasion, it can lead to an unexpected moment and memory between father and child. If we don't have a special movie, book, song, sports team, or TV show with our child, then we need to either target these areas during our structured time or increase our unstructured time and hope it happens. However, targeted, structured time is important. It shows our child that we have a willingness to work and improve the dad/child relationship. It shows intention. It shows priority. It is so important that the next two deposits (Deposits #2 and #3) focus on the many happy returns that may be reaped if we invest in positive structured time with our kids.

Whether structured or unstructured, get out there and spend time with your kid. Your dad/child checking account will thank you.

• MEGGIE'S TAKE •

Having shared experiences is important for any relationship, so of course it's important for kid/parent relationships. However, all this talk of ten thousand hours and spending more time with your child than the culture does is kind of terrifying to me as a kid. Sure, I want to see my parents, but do I want to hang out with them more than my friends? Nope. I'm also not convinced that more time spent with my dad will lead to a better relationship. It really depends on what we're doing with that time. Are we making fun memories, or do I feel like I'm being forced to spend time with my dad when I would rather be with my friends? I don't think the answer is just sheer amount of time spent.

Unless you're planning to force your kid to spend time with you, good luck reaching all those hours. I think that being intentional about the time you do spend, rather than just going for the hours, is going to make more of a long-term impact on your kid. That being said, I think there are small things you can do to show your kid you care about them and want to spend time with them without annoying them in the process. For example, if your kid is doing homework in the living room, you could be reading there too. Just don't be too omnipresent, or your kid will start to retreat at the weirdness of spending too much time with you.

Grade: B

DAD ACCOUNTABILITY HOMEWORK

Answer Y/N

1. For any day this week, did I spend more than one uninterrupted hour with my child? _____
2. During the weekend, did I spend more than two uninterrupted hours with my child? _____

22. RUN AWAY WITH YOUR CHILD: TAKE ONE MEMORABLE TRIP ALONE (DEPOSIT #2)

"Oh, Montana!" That's all he had to say to make his daughter smile and forget about whatever dispute or distance there was between them. It was and remains his go-to trump card to end any dispute with his daughter.

For the ultimate in structured time, take your child and run away for a week.

Now, for the rest of the Montana story.

About two decades ago, a veteran dad was sharing some advice with a new dad. The older dad spoke about the importance of doing a special, once-in-a-lifetime trip with each child before they went away to college or their first job. It was a very simple concept. Each child picked the destination (within reason), and the two of them went there. No mom. No siblings. No job. No school. It was just the two of them. He said it was magic, relationship gold.

The magic wasn't obvious to the new dad. He saw a week away as being expensive, putting him behind at work, and leaving his wife behind to deal with three other children without backup. Frankly, it seemed unnecessary and extravagant. It was not something that he ever did with his dad. None of his buddies ever did it with their dads. A father/child one-on-one vacation—who did such a thing? The older and wiser father persisted, "Try it with your oldest daughter. If it's a bust, then don't do it with the rest." He insisted there was nothing to lose and everything to gain. If it was truly magic, then it could be a rite of passage with each child.

Since the older father's children seemed to have their acts together, after consultation with his wife, the younger father decided to try it with his oldest daughter (age eleven) with measured expectations.

The father told his daughter to pick a place to go for a week, just the two of them. It was a topic of frequent conversation. They had fun talking about the pros and cons of various locations. They learned about different parts of the map. It always gave them something to talk about and debate. He was steering her to New York City or Washington, DC, so they could see a great American city and all that it had to offer. Maybe they could even take in a baseball game. Now *that* would be quality father/daughter time.

She listened but was noncommittal about the baseball adventure.

Finally, one morning she came bounding downstairs full of enthusiasm and declared, "Let's go to Montana and ride horses together."

He thought but did not say, *Montana? What about seeing the Mets play in New York City?* The fact was, he hadn't ridden a horse in thirty years, and that was very much on purpose. But there she was, staring upward at him, expectation in her eleven-year-old eyes. What could he do but declare, "Westward ho! Montana, here we come." And off they went, and it was magic from beginning to end.

The father learned that strange things happen when you take one child away from the family unit. The family dynamic completely changes. The child can't occupy her usual place (and attending behavior), be it as oldest, middle, or youngest child. When it's one-on-one time, there's no place to hide—for dad or child. Dad has to focus on the one kid and make something happen, or it's going to be a long week. The kid can't be quiet or inactive, bailed out by other, more active or talkative siblings. Initially, it's actually startling to be one on one with our child—definitely unfamiliar territory. But removing life's distractions and being one on one with our child is how the magic happens.

Opportunities and challenges are handled *together*. In Montana, someone had to hand-milk the baby calves, so they did it together. (Translation: The daughter did it while Dad watched.) The horses had to be ridden; the cattle fed, moved between fields, and branded. Some fences had to be mended. Sure, at times it all felt like a bad dream sequence based on the *City Slickers* movie, but they figured Montana out together.

This deposit is a no-brainer. It is fatherhood gold, the ultimate expression of Deposit #1 "Do It: The Deeds," combining both structured and unstructured time. The trip can be across the country or to a state park an hour away depending on time and budget considerations. It can be upscale or a camping trip. To each his own. The only key is to get away from the family unit. It is impossible to mess up, because of the law of "fatherhood comparative advantage." What this made-up law means is that so few of us will actually take a week-long one-on-one trip with our children that even if it turns out to be a C+ experience, it will become an A+ when graded on the curve of nonparticipation by the rest of the Disappearing Dads.

The Fun Factor—Part 1

The most important part of the trip together: FUN! The more fun, the larger the deposit. We all need to get out of our comfort zones and have fun (and maybe even be a bit silly) with our children. (Hint: Yell "Dance party," start dancing, and see what happens.)

Admission and Epilogue

Actually, the young father cheated, just a bit, but it luckily didn't cost him. He didn't really buy into the week-long concept, so he booked the Montana trip from Sunday to Thursday so he could be back in the office on Friday to handle any work-related issues that surfaced during the week.

More than a decade has passed since that Montana trip, and he shared that he has no idea what he did on that Friday back at work, but it cost him two days in Montana with his oldest daughter, who is now grown and on her own. They loved the trip, but he still feels a twinge of regret in missing those two days. And for what? A day at the office?

He never made that mistake again. For the rest of his children, it was the full-week experience. Oh, and child number three did select New York City, so he saw the Mets play after all.

We would all do well to abide the advice from the older father and carve our own "Montana moment." Happy trails! Have fun!

• MEGGIE'S TAKE •

Here's my question: Why do you care so much what your kid thinks about you? We're kids. We are going to complain and whine and think our parents are the WORST. It's part of our job description. We're not going to be able to view you with a clear head until we're deep into adulthood, if ever. So while I appreciate you wanting us to like you, I'm not sure why you're so concerned about the grade we're going to give you. News flash: It's probably not going to be an A.

Now, to be fair, the trip was pretty awesome and definitely tipped the scales a little bit when I was a kid. But I don't think it's quite the "no-brainer" you describe. It's a huge time-and-money commitment, and I don't think it's very realistic for a lot of people. The general principle of time spent together is a good one, and I don't think you have to take off an entire week of work to do that.

Grade: B

DAD ACCOUNTABILITY HOMEWORK

Answer and Date

1. Invite your child to pick the place. _____
2. Enjoy discussions on possible places. _____
3. Child picks the place. _____
4. You make the fun itinerary. _____
5. Where did you go? _____
6. Did you spend a full week? _____
7. Did your child have FUN? _____
8. Was it a bust or impactful? _____
9. Grade the experience. _____

If you feel so led, please join The Super Dad Myth Facebook community group and post your story (and a fun picture!) as inspiration for the next dad.

23. HAVE THAT "ONE THING" WITH YOUR KID (DEPOSIT #3)

Running away with your child is great, but time marches on, and structured time isn't over when we return home. We need to build on the trip and create more structured events that no one can take away. We need to find that elusive "one thing" that connects us. Here's how the "one thing" came about for my son and me.

At my son's first birthday party, his godfather approached me like a man on a mission. He invaded my personal space, made laser-beam eye contact, and whispered, "I have something to tell you."

"Sure, what's up?" I said.

After a dramatic pause and quick glance to make sure no one was listening, he continued, "Make sure that you have that *one thing* with your son. Got it?"

Got what? I thought. I didn't know what he was driving at, but to lighten the moment, I weakly offered, "Sure, sure . . . yeah . . . I totally gotcha on the 'one thing' thing. Covered. One thing, two things, whatever it takes."

Godfather was not amused at my lame *Mr. Mom* movie reference. He stiffened and repeated, "I'm not talking about two things. I'm talking about having that *one thing*. Capice?"

Capice? I was still not tracking, so I asked him straight up, "Okay, what exactly is the *one thing* I have to have with my son?"

Godfather rolled his eyes in exasperation. "How would I know? It's *your* one thing, not mine!"

Now I was frustrated, feeling stupid, and somewhat annoyed, so I tensely asked, "What are we talking about here? What do you mean by the *one thing*?"

"It's the one thing that *belongs to just you and your son*, and no one else."

"It belongs to just us . . . hmm . . . all right, that makes some sense, but I'm not there yet. Give me an example. What is your *one thing* with your son?"

"Oh, that's easy."

But he stopped and didn't answer further, so I prodded, "Well, what is it?"

"That's the wrong question."

"It is? What's the right question?"

"Whether the *one thing* is real. Isn't that really what you want to know?"

"Okay, yes. I suppose I want to know both. I want to know, what is your *one thing* with your son, and is it real?"

Godfather seemed pleased that I was understanding, even though I still wasn't sure what was going on. "If you want to know if the *one thing* is real, who should you be asking?"

After a moment, the lightbulb slowly went off in my head. "Your son?"

"Exactly right. If he can't answer the questions, then you will know that the *one thing* is a fraud."

I nodded and searched out his son, almost hoping to expose the fraud. I startled him with my quick approach and asked, "Your dad mentioned that you two have a thing. Actually, *one thing*. Does that sound familiar to you?"

The son smiled and replied, "Sure does."

"You mind telling me what your *one thing* is?"

His son leaned in, as if sharing state secrets, and in a hushed tone said, "It's golf."

"Golf?"

"Yeah, once or twice a month we play golf together. Sometimes we pick up another twosome, but mostly it's just the two of us. No matter what is going on, we never miss our golf match."

Frankly, I was underwhelmed, having been expecting something much more profound. I went back over to my son's godfather to tell him that his whole *one thing* didn't exactly impress. "Golf? That's the one thing? That's it?"

"Exactly right," he said with a wide smile.

"I gotta say, it doesn't exactly move the meter," I said. "I prefer sports that when I hit the ball, someone else has to chase it. Is that the best you got?"

"I think you misunderstand," he told me. "Our *one thing* isn't hitting a small ball into a small hole. For us, once or twice a month, we put everything else aside and spend four to six hours together outdoors, usually alone, but sometimes we pick up a twosome if the course is crowded. Sometimes we talk a little, sometimes a lot. Regardless of the circumstances, we are available to each other. The time together and game itself teach many life lessons, like playing alone, playing with strangers, patience, success, failure, competition, and sportsmanship, all under my watchful eye. No matter what troubles exist—either between us or with others—they tend to fade during our regular golf matches. Regardless of life's difficulties, it's hard not to celebrate the moment when your son hits a big drive or drains a twenty-footer. And it's hard not to look forward to our next golf outing."

My immediate thought was his spouse must see right through this *one thing* scam as being nothing but a clever excuse to play golf. Yet, his spouse didn't suffer fools easily and was frankly the brains of the operation, so it wasn't that. This had her blessing. I had to concede that maybe this structured *one thing* stuff was real.

The Fun Factor—Part 2

Reminder for us slow learners: Having fun with our kids is essential to deposit making. Play golf, or tennis, or music, or video games, or pursue some common interest. Anything! Don't misunderstand—we're not trying to be their "best friend" or "buddy." We'll keep the father role, thank you very much. Yet by doing fun things, we are affirming and cementing the relationship. Let's not be stiffs. HAVE. FUN. NOW!

• MEGGIE'S TAKE •

Oh, Dad, you're going down hard on this one. At the risk of sounding salty, is this just for sons? I know my memory is bad, but I don't think it's bad enough to forget our *one thing*. Now, don't get me wrong—I think this is a great idea. Are you speaking from experience on this one, though? I don't think so . . .

Grade: A (for idea)
      F (for execution)

DAD ACCOUNTABILITY HOMEWORK

                                                           Answer and Date

1. What is the one thing?   _____
2. When did you first do it?   _____
3. How long did you keep it going?   _____
4. Has it been a bust or impactful?   _____
5. Grade the experience.   _____

If you feel so led, please join The Super Dad Myth Facebook community group and post your story (and a fun picture!) as inspiration for the next dad.

24. SAY IT! THE THREE MOST POWERFUL WORDS (DEPOSIT #4)

The Three Most Powerful Words — Part 1: "I Love You"

Showing love by investing your time is superior to spouting meaningless words. To say we love our children but then ignore them is cruel hypocrisy. How about we make our words reinforce our deeds?

Our children talk about their feelings and emotions much more than prior generations. Today's children are encouraged to be vulnerable and transparent. They are told to go beyond the surface and invest deeply in authentic relationships. For many of us dads, these are foreign concepts. Feelings? Emotions? Vulnerabilities? Why would we share our weaknesses with others, or even acknowledge them to ourselves? But times have changed. Clint Eastwood's "get off my lawn" character portrayal in the movie *Gran Torino* is no longer the standard-bearer for manhood or relational connectedness.

There is a chilling reality in our futures. Our college-aged children confided in us that in discussions with their peer group, they ultimately got around to the "dad topic." They talk about their dads. They evaluate how we did our dad jobs. Simply put, in the near future, our fatherhood will be put on trial by our children and their peers (though they won't admit it, of course). The verdict will be a Caesar-like thumbs-up or thumbs-down.

For many of us, we've been distant while pursuing our own interests. Especially with our daughters, we've sometimes been acquaintances in the same household, minding our own business. But there is hope. While our *deeds* remain the primary evidence, the youthful jury will generally focus on one piece of exculpatory evidence that can save us from a thumbs-down verdict. The peer group will turn, face the witness (our child), and ask one make-or-break question: Did your father say "I love you" while you were growing up?

Bam! There it is. That is the question. This is the moment. Did we actually say *the three words*? Did we at least write it in a note or letter to our children, or did we completely cop out? If our child testifies "yes," then we're in the clear. The three words forgive a multitude of parental errors and omissions (within reason), and the thumbs-up verdict is rendered. Happy days!

On the other hand, what if the answer is "no," and for whatever reason we never could quite spit out "I love you"? There is still hope, but we just made our lives harder—much harder. If we refuse to say it, then we have to *do more deeds* that express what we refuse to say.

Let's quantify the challenge. If we won't say it, then we have only one way to get a favorable verdict: We have to be an A+ deed dad. Not easy! Here is the grid:

	Deeds	Words	Grade	Verdict
Very Active but Silent	A	F	C	👍
Mostly Active but Silent	B	F	D	👎
Inactive and Silent	F	F	F	👎
Very Active and Says the Words	A	A	A	👍
Slacker but Says the Words	C	A	B	👍
Inactive but Says the Words	F	A	C	👎

It really doesn't seem fair. A dad that grades out as a C in deeds but an A in words (by sincerely saying "I love you" to his children on a regular basis) is in the clear, while another dad who grades out as a B in deeds but doesn't say the words may not make the grade? Yup, but that is the power of sincerely saying the three words, provided a minimal level of deeds exist to support the words. If we're not willing to say them, then we better have an A in deeds. Even then, we're still a full letter grade behind the semi-slacker deed dads who say "I love you" to their children.

As the grid reveals, the three words are valuable. If we are frequent in sincerely saying "I love you" to our children, they will give us a *deeds discount*—the key word being *discount*. It is not a license to ignore doing deeds and cross the line into hypocrisy. If we are inactive dads, saying "I love you" won't make a difference. But for the slacker dad who wants to play some golf or carve out a little "me time" on the weekends, then the words, if sincere, can provide the workable margin for just such a balance—within reason.

On the flip side, if we can't bring ourselves to say the three words, we get no deeds discount. Instead, the deeds bill must be paid in full. So put away the golf clubs and forget about watching back-to-back football games on Sunday. No, we have chosen a different path. We will be listening to piano practices, attending recitals, playing house, staying with our children at birthday parties, volunteering to take down the set for the high school play, and so many other things that the slacker "I love you" dads never have to deal with. That is the lot our silence has chosen. Some strong, silent–type dads may protest, saying that just isn't their way. Nice try, but words matter too. Withholding professions of love to our children doesn't show strength. To the contrary, it confirms weakness.

Now, there are exceptions. Some fathers don't actually love their children (it happens), so not saying the three words makes sense. It's logical. The relationship is more transactional. The young are cared for in youth and the elderly cared for in old age. It's not very inspirational, but the biological baton is passed and the family tree extended. Frankly, such fathers may be tempted to say the three words if for no other reason than to get the deeds discount. But they don't. Such scenarios are sad, but not saying the three words is perversely understandable in such circumstances. This is a thumbs-down scenario all the way.

A different sadness is the number of fathers who deeply love their children, yet never say the three words. Too many of our children have to report to their peer group, "My father never said he loved me," or "My father never hugged me." An unspoken profession of love becomes a mystery to our children. They ponder, *If my father did love me, why didn't he ever say the simple words?* Their minds can wander into the emotionally unhealthy territory of, *Maybe he didn't love me.*

Is that what we want our children thinking? Do we want to go down in history as the austere father?

The Three Most Powerful Words—Part 2: "I Am Sorry"

Despite our best efforts at doing positive deeds and frequently saying "I love you" to foster a joyous father/child relationship, there will be conflict;

there always is. But part of being an effective dad is being a *dogged reconciler*. Children have an amazing capacity to think they know more than they do. They get it from their parents. As parents, we think we know more than we do. Therefore, conflict is inevitable, as both parties have inflated views of their respective infallibility. There will be arguments about both serious and silly things. And standoffs. And dirty looks. And pouting. And silent treatments. It comes with the territory.

But there must be reconciliation! And quickly, to prevent a manageable dispute from festering into full-blown conflict and relational isolation. The power of a timely apology is strong, but too many of us choose not to use that power.

Without reconciliation, our children are pushed away from us and closer to the culture (and its influence)—the opposite of what we want to accomplish. As parents, we are supposed to be the "adults in the room," the peacekeepers. That doesn't mean we cave to all teenager demands just to keep the peace, but it does mean that we should be humble enough (and for dads, man enough) to recognize when we are in the wrong, and then go to our children, apologize, and ask for their forgiveness. This is tough for some of us, as apologizing to our children—or sometimes anyone—just isn't in our DNA. But we need to get over ourselves. We need to be smart and recognize the three most powerful words to be a dogged reconciler: *I am sorry*.

When we're in the wrong, or partially in the wrong, rather than stubbornly hold on to our shaky arguments, we need to set our pride aside and eat a heaping portion of humble pie. We're not perfect dads, so quit pretending. Let's apologize when we're wrong and quickly reconcile with our children. And don't think an apology will shock our children. They already think we're wrong and know we're not perfect. Just ask them. Also, do the apology right. Don't qualify it. Don't use weasel words like, "I did nothing wrong and still believe that I'm right, but if the real-world wisdom I shared caused your overly sensitive, immature feelings to be hurt, then I'm sorry."

No. Go all in with the apology. Almost go overboard with it, but don't cross the line of insincerity. Confess to being 100 percent wrong and having completely mishandled the situation. Give your child no room to criticize the apology. Show fierce strength in your weakness. Why? Because if you mess up the apology, it will throw gas on the original dispute and return it to a boil rather than a cooled reconciliation.

Besides, if we don't apologize when we are wrong, how will our children know what to do when they are wrong? If we never apologize to our children, do we really think they will? If we don't show forgiveness, how will we ever receive it? It's stunning how many of us have never apologized to our children—*for anything*—as if we're perfect dads. Yet we're surprised when our children will not apologize to us when they are in the wrong. Self-deception and hypocrisy reign.

What about when we're clearly right and our children are clearly wrong? It's rare, but it can happen. We still need to be a dogged reconciler. But how? First, the easy out is to examine *materiality*. Is the subject of the dispute material enough to fight over in the first place? Are we arguing about the propriety of recreational drug use or the rules when playing Monopoly? If the fight is about recreational drug use, then stay strong. If the fight arises while playing Monopoly, it's not worth it. Cave fast and hard, finish the game, and have some fun. As a parent, we have limited deposits in the dad/child checking account, so let's save them for the big issues and not waste them on meaningless quarrels.

Second, in a minority of cases where we are clearly in the right and the dispute is material, we probably have no choice but to risk conflict and make a *withdrawal* from the dad/child checking account. This is never easy, and it is impossible if you have a near-zero balance in the account.

For instance, if our high schoolers assert that recreational marijuana use is acceptable in their peer group, that qualifies as a big issue. As dads, many of us could not cave to that thinking and would oppose it, even if it brought conflict—and conflict it will bring. Our children will argue that there is no difference between a parent's recreational alcohol drinking and their recreational pot use. Parents will oppose that view with various arguments. Gridlock and raised voices ensue. This is a critical juncture. Before tempers overflow, take a break. Cool down and return to dialogue, focusing on playing your two key dad cards: (1) recognition of fallibility, and (2) getting credit for prior deposits.

Playing the Two Dad Cards: Fallibility and Credit for Prior Deposits

Let's tell our children straight up that while many of our decisions have been right, we're going to make a few dud decisions along the way. Some real stinkers. All families live with the parental decisions, good and bad. That's the human condition. Let's own our fallibility and set realistic expectations.

Going back to the drug example. We simply tell our child that recreational pot use is not a winning strategy for success. We're not only against it; we forbid it, no exceptions. Then admit that we may be wrong, apologize in advance for that potential, and have that be the end of it—the last word.

Sounds nice, but does that strategy work? Will our children say, "Oh sure, Dad. Now I get it. Recreational pot smoking is bad and I'll be sure to tell my peer group"? Hardly. But does the argument have to drone on or escalate to a shouting match? That depends on the second dad card: getting credit for prior deposits. Sometimes, our last resort is to remind our children of the Montana trip, or of all the times they were told "I love you," or all the fun times together. We must remind them of our positive account balance, and it is time for a small withdrawal. Sometimes it works, other times it doesn't. Even when it doesn't work, we need to stand for the truth as we see it. If our children defy our guidance and smoke pot on a recreational basis, they will know they are going against the family guidance. They will have to sneak around. They will have to act below the family standard. Their poor choices will cause hardship and may even lead to personal destruction. It happens even in the most loving family environments. Yet we must love them through it. In fact, although very difficult, telling and showing our children "I love you" is probably more important when their behavior is below the family standard.

We all know or have heard of some dad who is estranged from a child over some issue. Maybe they haven't spoken in years. One wonders, "Was it worth it?" Was the pride of holding on to the original beef and not using the three most powerful words worth the relational brokenness? How sad.

Instead, let's be dogged reconcilers. Be humble. Do no harm.

For many of us, it's time to man up. If you love your children, tell them in a direct way. Tell them now—right now! Not tomorrow, next week, next month, next year, or on your deathbed. Right now!

Stop reading! Do not resume until the words have been said!

Welcome back.

For those dads who actually said the words for the first time (5 percent, maybe), that was TOUGH. The good news is that it gets easier and easier.

Deeds matter, but so do words. Talk is not cheap, and failing to profess the three words to our children is cowardly. Oh, and while we're at it, why not say "I love you" to our wives *in front of our children?* A twofer. But more on that later.

> ### • MEGGIE'S TAKE •
>
> My friends and I have occasionally talked about our dads. But we never sat down to have this supposed "dad talk." Any comments were made in passing, and no one EVER asked, "Did your dad ever tell you he loved you?" This apparent "get out of jail free" card never even came up. That doesn't mean it isn't important to tell your kids you love them (I think it definitely is), but in terms of the peer-to-peer "thumbs up," I'm not sure this is quite the deciding factor you think it is.
>
> Also, if you're saying "I love you" as a way to get a "discount," I think you've got the wrong idea. Are you trying to get out of your kid's recitals, practices, parties, and volunteering? At that point, it won't matter how much you tell them you love them; your kid will be disappointed. If you ever make it even seem like you want to watch pro football all day instead of going to little Jimmy's soccer game, good luck to you.
>
> Grade: C

DAD ACCOUNTABILITY HOMEWORK

	Check One	
	Yes	No
1. Have you ever said "I love you" to your child?	_____	_____
2. Do you weekly say "I love you" to your child?	_____	_____

Work hard to answer "yes" to both questions. This is very personal; no posting to the Facebook group on this one.

25. AFFIRMATION > CORRECTION 10:1 RATIO (DEPOSIT #5)

The first four deposits lead to many happy father-child experiences to be forever cherished. Another benefit is that such positive experiences also earn us the opportunity to more effectively *correct* our children. We admit the verb "earn" may rub some old-school parents the wrong way, as we don't have to earn the right to correct our children; it is an inherent right arising from our status as their parents. Point taken. And again, we're not trying to be our child's buddy. Our only point is that if we positively build the relationship, then our children may be more open to more correction—some of the time. If we don't, they won't, and we'll have to rely on the parental status to practice correction. If we don't blow it, our children are open to correction, particularly in the areas of "safety, morality, and social rules" according to Jennifer Wallace.[96]

The quickest way to blow it and lose our parental influence is to constantly correct and infrequently praise our kids. Not false praise, but sincere praise for good behaviors or positive character traits. Too many of us jump at the chance to correct the slightest infraction, but are slow to affirm obedience or positive behaviors. Too many of us are insufferably self-righteous. Too many of us are parental curmudgeons that are tuned out because of overcorrection and under-fun. The real shame is that we should know better. This message has been packaged (and repackaged) since biblical times.

"Why do you look at the speck of sawdust in your brother's eye and pay no attention to the plank in your own eye? How can you say to your brother, 'Let me take the speck out of your eye,' when all the time there is a plank in your own eye? You hypocrite, first take the plank out of your own eye, and then you will see clearly to remove the speck from your brother's eye" (Matthew 7:3–5, NIV).

For the more secularly inclined, in Dale Carnegie's classic book *How to Win Friends and Influence People*, the very first chapter is titled, "If You Want to Gather Honey, Don't Kick Over the Beehive." (Translation: Never criticize anyone ever.) Carnegie goes back to founding father Ben Franklin, and sums up the secret of Franklin's success: "I will speak ill of no man . . . and speak all the good I know of everybody."[97]

Carnegie admits he was slow to learn this lesson in his own life: "I personally had to blunder through this old world for a third of a century before it even began to dawn upon me that ninety-nine times out of a hundred, no man ever criticizes himself for anything, no matter how wrong he may be."[98]

Many of us never learn this lesson, inside or outside our homes. People are influenced by those who affirm them.

In his 2016 book *The Name of God Is Mercy*, Pope Francis added that not only should men not speak ill of one another, but they should seek out "every single possible way to forgive" and restore relationships. Pope Francis then tells a story from the novel *To Every Man a Penny*, where a young priest sought to provide absolution to a condemned German soldier about to be put to death. The soldier "confesses his passion for women and the numerous amorous adventures he has had." The priest implored the soldier to repent his sins and seek forgiveness before death. The soldier replied, "How can I repent? It was something I enjoyed and if I had the chance I would do it again, even now." Being desperate to save the soldier's soul, the priest thought and thought and finally had a breakthrough and asked, "But are you sorry that you are not sorry?" The soldier thought for a moment and replied, "Yes, I am sorry that I am not sorry." Pope Francis explains that the soldier's "sorrow is the opening that allows the merciful priest to give the man absolution."[99]

The point of the story is not the German soldier; it's the priest's creative efforts to bring forgiveness and eternal restoration to the soldier. How many of us are being that creative to find ways to affirm our children?

The 10:1 Affirmation/Correction Ratio

So how often do we need to affirm our children before they will be receptive to correction? In his book *Practicing Affirmation*, Sam Crabtree puts forth a ratio of ten affirmations for every one correction.[100] Crabtree writes, "Affirming others earns us the right standing from which to make suggestions. It gains us a hearing."[101]

Can we achieve such a robust ratio? Probably not. But at a minimum we need to make sure we have a *positive* ratio. Too many of us have a negative ratio—we correct more than we affirm—and then wonder why our correction is so ineffective, leading to constant squabbling. Like the young priest, let's be creative in finding ways to sincerely affirm our children and thereby create an opening for later corrections. Making the first four deposits is just a starting point. We all need to think creatively to be an affirming, more effective parent.

• MEGGIE'S TAKE •

There's nothing I hated more as a kid than when Mom or Dad told me to do something "because I said so." And you better believe I was thinking, *You have no idea how well-behaved I am! Especially compared to my peers! You're so lucky, and all you can do is get mad at me for doing this one tiny little thing wrong!*

In my mind, this is just bad kid management. Sure, you may be able to make us do the right thing by playing your "dad" card. But this goes back to a point I've made before and I'm sure I'll make again: If I don't know why I'm not supposed to be doing something, it won't last once Mom or Dad isn't around to tell me not to anymore.

I like the message that you bring up with this Bible verse (although you only implied it, not stated it, so you only get half credit). Parents are hypocrites. So are we all. But if you are over here trying to tell me to forgive everyone, but then you are still holding a grudge against that neighbor who did that thing that one time, how much am I, as a kid, going to want to listen to you? If you say not to gossip about other people, but make no effort to stop gossiping yourself . . . you've lost your credibility with me!

It's my firm belief that you can always find something genuine to compliment someone else on. There's no need for false affirmation. When you switch your mindset to see the positive, I think that's better for everyone. So I like this message (except your interpretation of Carnegie's quote, which is why you got an A-). In some ways, kids are no different than adults. We all want to know that we are appreciated. Both kids and adults need to do better at showing that appreciation to others.

Grade A-

DAD ACCOUNTABILITY HOMEWORK

For this past week: Answer and Date

1. Did you affirm your child?   _____
2. How many times?   _____
3. What specific behavior or value
   did you affirm?   _____
4. Did you correct your child?   _____
5. How many times?   _____
6. What specific behavior or value
   did you correct?   _____
7. Did you affirm more than correct?   _____
8. If yes, is this repeatable?   _____
9. Is this deposit working or a bust?   _____

If you feel so led, please join The Super Dad Myth Facebook community group and post your affirmation story (and a fun picture!) as inspiration for the next dad.

26. LOVE THE MOTHER (BUCKET #2)

BUCKET FILLING

Deposit #6   Leave your Crown in the garage

Deposit #7   Honor and Respect
               our Children's Mother

At one time or another nearly all dads have thought, *I'm a better father than I am a husband.* It's a rational thought. After all, it's hard to get into an argument about money or the urgent need to replace drapes with plantation shutters with a three-year-old cutie in ribbons staring back at you. Reality-check time: We can't be good fathers if we're consistently son-of-a-gun, know-it-all, domineering, lousy husbands (or ex-husbands) to the mother of our children. We need to get our own houses in order with the next two deposits.

27. LEAVE YOUR SUCCESS CROWN IN THE GARAGE (DEPOSIT #6)

If you are reading this book, you're probably a resourced person. You probably have a good education. You have formed a functioning household. Your kids go to good schools. Your family goes on vacation most years. You make decent money, more than most. Maybe you're a celebrity, executive, professor, doctor, cop, lawyer, pastor, leader, influencer, or some dude generally acclaimed by the culture. You have earned the world's crown of success.

If you want to be a better dad, here's a tip from a lady: Leave your "success crown" in the garage—so says one of the most accomplished women in the world, Indra Nooyi.

Nooyi was born in India, where she would later earn her undergraduate degree. She earned her master's degree from the Yale School of Management. After working as a business consultant, she joined PepsiCo in 1994. By 2006, she was PepsiCo's president and chief executive officer, responsible for leading more than 250,000 global employees. She was the top boss for twelve years. During her tenure, total shareholder return was 149 percent (compared with 197 percent at Coca-Cola), and PepsiCo was worth $165 billion, according to the *Wall Street Journal*.[102] Nooyi earned the acclaim of the international business world. In 2016 alone, Nooyi's total compensation was $29.8 million.[103] In 2017, she was named the second most powerful woman in the business world, according to *Fortune* magazine.[104]

She has money. She has power. She has prestige. She is a person of great privilege and status. She has a very large success crown.

But don't mention the crown to Nooyi's mother.

Nooyi was named PepsiCo's president one evening. She rushed home to tell her mother and family, but the celebratory coronation didn't happen. In Nooyi's retelling, the story took an unexpected turn:

> I went home and said, "Mom, I have some very important news." To which she said, "Leave that very important news, just go buy some milk." To which I said, "Raj is home. Why don't you ask him to buy the milk?" She said, "He is tired." Typical mother, you know, can't disturb the son-in-law! I was upset, but I went and bought the milk and banged it on the kitchen table in front of her and said, "Tell me, why do I have to buy the milk and not somebody else?" She just looked at me—and I will never forget it, and it was a powerful lesson she left in me, and said, "You might be the president of PepsiCo. You might be on the board of directors. But when you enter this house, you're the wife, the daughter, the daughter-in-law, the mother. You're all of that. Nobody else can take that place. So leave that damned crown in the garage.

And don't bring it into the house." You know I've never seen that crown.[105, 106]

Nooyi's been married to the same guy for nearly forty years and has two stable and productive daughters. Why? Probably for a lot of reasons, but it didn't hurt that she had the wisdom to leave her success crown in the garage and not shirk her other roles. She did not confuse workplace success with family and home-life success. Both require effort and patience. She had the humility to swallow her pride and "buy the milk" when directed by her mother. Perhaps we can benefit our families by living humbly, making the late-night milk runs, and leaving our darned crowns in the garage before entering our homes.

• MEGGIE'S TAKE •

Success and privilege are two different things, and I think you are conflating the two here. Privilege often leads to success, or makes success more attainable. Both concepts certainly apply to the lesson you are teaching here, which is humility. It is important to recognize the privileges that you have, because they put your "success" into perspective. Once you realize all the ways you have been privileged, you can view your own success with humility because you recognize that your privileges helped you get there. We rarely (if ever) do things entirely on our own merit, and I think it is important to recognize the role your privilege plays in getting you where you are.

I think kids often imitate what their parents do, so showing humility rather than just talking about it is key. That's what I like about this lesson. However, I think that taking that same humility out into the world is also critical. In my opinion, it's just as important to make sure that when you do go back into the garage, put the crown on, and go into the world, you're not losing the humility you cultivated with your family.

Grade: B+

DAD ACCOUNTABILITY HOMEWORK

Pick a disfavored household chore (lawn, dishes, trash, bathroom duty, whatever) and instead of delegating it, make it your own. It's hard for our children to shirk their chores when they see Dad cleaning toilets or making late-night milk runs.

                                                            Answer and Date

1. What chore did you pick?   _____
2. How long did you stick with it?   _____
3. Is this deposit working or a bust? _____

If you feel so led, please join The Super Dad Myth Facebook community group and post your story (and a fun picture!) as inspiration for the next dad.

28. HONOR AND RESPECT OUR CHILDREN'S MOTHER (DEPOSIT #7)

It's a funny thing, but our children tend to really love their mothers. Our children tend to spend more time with their mothers talking, confiding in, and having their immediate needs met. If they had to choose between us and their mothers, well, let's not go down that road. So being a jerk to the very person who gave our children life is a losing proposition—always has been and always will be. Yet many of us are extremely slow learners.

No one said this deposit would always be easy. This one makes saying "I love you" to our kids look like a walk in the park. For many of us, this will be the hardest deposit to consistently put in the dad/child checking account, and the reason is simple. As husbands, we're always right, and when our spouses don't see our brilliance, conflict naturally follows. We get upset; we may even raise our voices to emphasize our correctness, but, surprisingly, the vocal emphasis never works.

Did we mention we are slow learners?

But there may be times—just a few—when we actually *are* right. It does happen, but for whatever reason, our spouses can't see it and take a 180-degree contrarian view. We're at a crossroads. If logic and vocal emphasis won't work, what will? There is a way out. It's simple, but not easy. At the moment of being a jerk (which is a huge withdrawal, not a deposit), we need to utter two simple, saving words: "Yes, dear." Then stop talking and hold fast to the silence. Keep holding. Keep holding! Say nothing. For any additional incoming volleys, simply repeat, "Yes, dear," and hold on some more.

It is amazing how many fires can be avoided by not putting gasoline on the flames. How many arguments in front of the children could have been avoided by just staying silent? By not giving the arguments oxygen? Sometimes, as husbands, we need to lead by *shutting up!*

Does this mean we have to be patsies and always give in to keep the marital peace? Of course not. But husbands and wives both make mistakes, so let's take turns and keep the mistake-making roughly equal. When we say "Yes, dear," we're merely saying in secret husband code, "Okay, you're dead wrong and this is a mistake, but I love you. I've made some mistakes, so now it's your turn."

Now, if we were right and it turned out to be a mistake, then we're simply keeping the "mistake ledger" equal. On the other hand, if our spouses turned out to be right, then we can take credit for having the good judgment to follow their views. Either way, we win, because we were not jerks to our wives in front of our children, and therefore avoided a large withdrawal from the dad/child checking account.

Dads, forget about your wives for a moment. If we fail to consistently honor them, we're again only hurting *ourselves*! First, we selfishly want a happy home life, which will be elusive if our spouses are not honored. Second, we selfishly want solid future daughters-in-law and sons-in-law, not duds that suck the life out of us. We want them to support us in our old age, not the other way around. If our children witness consistent marital infighting and strife, then that is what marriage looks like to them. That is their normal. They will date quarrelsome women. They will marry contentious men. Why wouldn't they? That is the marriage we modeled, and they learned the lessons. How sad if we set the marital bar so low for our children when searching for their own life partners.

We need to flip the script. Instead of barely clearing a low bar by not doing bad things (i.e. avoiding the jerk factor), why not aim high and maximally honor our wives by doing good things (the gallant factor)? Gallant means brave, courageous, giving *special attention and respect to women*. What if we could be gallant husbands to our wives for our daughters to witness? What if our daughters could see glimpses of what gallantry really looked like? What if we went so far as to regularly and whimsically tell our wives that we love them *in front of our children*? Sure, there will be an eye roll (nothing new there), but isn't that a lesson in gallantry that our children won't forget?

Okay, okay, maybe that goes too far. But is there any reason we couldn't take baby steps to express gallantry to our wives, witnessed by our children? How about we begin by minimizing *physical separateness* from our wives? At some point along the way, many of us stopped being hand-in-hand marital couples and turned into parental tag-team partners, tending (usually separately) to the constant demands of family life, but never in the ring together. Multiple children and their conflicting activities and schedules require a "divide and conquer" parental response that separates many couples. This can go on for years. But we can take steps to break the "divide and conquer" cycle without neglecting the kids. When it's family movie night, the parents sit next to each other. At church, at the ball game, the birthday party, the family reunion, wherever, make it standard practice to sit next to your wife. This is a small act. We're not exactly storming the castle and rescuing damsels in distress, but it is a step in the right direction on the gallantry path.

Over time, the example of *marital nearness* takes hold and makes an impression on our children. The best part—even better than enhancing our marriage and modeling a favorable view of marriage for our children—is that living a life of marital nearness is completely free of charge. There's an old adage that "women marry men like their fathers." Now, that's a scary thought. Yet, if we want our daughters to reject the jokers and jesters, then we better show them what gallant princes look like and how future queens are to be treated. We're going to fall short most of the time, but if we could meet the mark at least some of the time, our children would benefit from such a glimpse. The choice to model is ours: Be gallant or not? Be prince or jester? Embrace marital nearness or remain distant? If we behave like the fool, the jerk, or the distant husband in front of our children, then we shouldn't be surprised when our future sons-in-law and daughters-in-law look a lot like us, in all our ungallant splendor and marital gloom.

• MEGGIE'S TAKE •

This section strikes me as all about keeping up appearances. Again, why do you care so much what your kids think? No one is denying that treating your wife right is a good thing, but you shouldn't just be doing it in front of the kids, right? This is a tough one for me to respond to because I'm not married, so I have no idea what I'm talking about here. But I'm wondering if it wouldn't be more beneficial for your kids to see you and your spouse having productive disagreements instead of slinking off to the closet to yell at each other. Kids are way more perceptive than you think, and your walls are probably thinner than you think too.

You also made the point that kids often marry people like their mother or father. If all they've seen of marital conflict is you and your spouse distantly yelling, your kids probably won't know how to resolve conflicts in their own relationships. You've talked a lot in this book about how kids model off their parents. I personally don't agree that just "staying quiet" during an argument, or else yelling it out, are the most productive models for your kids. But then again, I wouldn't know. I'm still just a kid myself.

Grade: C

DAD ACCOUNTABILITY HOMEWORK

Pick one task you can consistently do to honor your spouse. (Ideas? Make the bed, make the coffee, open the car door, leave her love notes, unload the dishwasher, pray with her, insist on sitting next to her at all meals, whatever.) You figure it out, she's your spouse.

Answer and Date

1. What task did you pick?   _____
2. How long did you stick with it?   _____
3. Has it changed your relationship?   _____

If you feel so led, please join The Super Dad Myth Facebook community group and post your story (and a fun picture!) as inspiration for the next dad.

29. SERVE OTHERS (BUCKET #3)

BUCKET FILLING

Deposit #8   Serve others today

Many of us live in our comfortable, predictable bubbles—and stray little. In the bubble, our children experience a life unimaginable even one generation ago. American society has largely moved beyond the basics of clean water, plentiful food, adequate shelter, safer neighborhoods, and decent schools. Our children—and the rest of us—now have *technology*. With smartphones, we can communicate with a person across the globe and ignore the person or situation in front of us. Oh, and most everything works instantly, so we have little tolerance for friction-filled experiences. Progress.

What's the big deal here? We already contribute to the social safety net by paying our taxes and putting our envelope in the church collection plate. Why must we serve others today? What's the payoff to our children to serve others?

Wake up—someday *we may be the others*. If we want our children to take care of us when we're old, rather than warehouse us in the local nursing home, we better instill in them a desire to serve others. But that's the payoff for us, not them. The payoff of serving others as a habit of daily life includes (1) not being so darned self-absorbed and, frankly, ungrateful and unhappy people lacking perspective; (2) not being indifferent to community needs; and (3) being able to experience the joy of serving. To benefit from serving others, we must fight to get out of our bubbles.

30. SERVE OTHERS TODAY (DEPOSIT #8)

When it comes to service, there are three types of people: (1) those who serve others; (2) those served by others; and (3) neither—those who keep to themselves, stay on the sidelines, and neither serve much nor receive much. In the family context, it's hard to stay on the sidelines. There are givers and takers. Family members who continually need help and those who continually provide it. In a letter providing encouragement to his friend James Monroe, who was distressed over a family situation, Thomas Jefferson reminded him of "Virginia's long-standing code of family honor: Those that can, do."[107] It has always been this way. What will we be within our families and to the wider community: the serving or the served?

Teenagers naturally struggle with nonservice to others for three reasons: (1) a selfish nature, (2) they follow our lead of nonservice, and (3) service has been reduced to check-the-box tasks rather than a habit of daily life. Let's unpack each reason.

As more fully developed in Chapter 6, we all have a selfish nature. We can't help ourselves in helping ourselves. We are very good at serving our own—namely, helping our kids get a leg up to a successful future—which is really only helping ourselves since their achievement is a feather in our own ego caps.

Second, when it comes to serving others, nearly all of us are on the sidelines. Between serving our employers, our families, and having a little "me time," there is no margin to serve others, even if we were so inclined, which we're not. How many of us are really willing to serve others if it requires a significant sacrifice to our lifestyles? (Any hands raised? I didn't think so.) Our teenagers follow our example of nonservice.

Third, our teenagers live in a culture of "mandatory volunteerism," which reduces community service to a task to be completed, not a habit to be repeated. Most high schools encourage volunteer community service as part of a student's college application. Others require it. For example, Maryland requires seventy-five volunteer community-service hours in order to graduate from high school. We have created a culture of "mandatory volunteerism," where the volunteer, as much as the recipient, receives the benefit. Brilliant!

Our children are good at playing the mandatory (or strongly encouraged) volunteering game. They visit the nursing home to comfort the elderly. Check. Assist at the local food bank to serve the hungry. Check. Participate in the monthly Beta Club service project. Check. Why? To serve others, or to serve themselves and their college applications? They go off to college and the volunteering stops. At home? They refuse to do their minimal chores. After all, there is no box to check for walking the dog or unloading the dishwasher.

What's the solution? How do we instill in our children (and ourselves) a desire to serve others as a habit of daily life? Realistically, it's tough.

This is not a fun, easy deposit like taking our kid away on a Montana trip. Our nature (our heart) commands that we serve ourselves, not others. That is why "mandatory volunteerism" came about in the first place. Absent the spiritual answer in Part II, the best we can do is employ three secular tools that will probably make service to others a bit more consistent, but fall short of being a habit of daily life.

The first tool is to *model it* for our children. Grand gestures are unrealistic. Start small. Take personal inventory. For those that have more money than time, give money. For those short on cash, give your time. Simple everyday acts of kindness will suffice. Serving others is graded pass/fail, not on a bell curve.

Start with the low-hanging fruit by looking for opportunities around the house. When was the last time we dads made our seventeen-year-old's bed? (Try never.) How often do we fold the laundry? (See prior response.) How often do we do the dishes? (See prior response.) How often do we attend our teenager's mandatory community-service projects? (Don't want to hover.) How often do we pick up a stray piece of trash in the neighborhood? (Not my trash.) How often do we help a neighbor going through a hard time? (Don't want to pry.) How often do we model doing the grunt work around the house and in the neighborhood? The more we model serving others, the more our children will see what it looks like. Will they copy what they see? Of course not, not at first. But they no longer have the easy out of copying our nonservice.

The second tool is *gratitude*. Many of us have a pretty good life going.

Sure, we gripe some, but deep down we know we have it pretty good, especially compared to others. A grateful heart typically causes us to want to serve others, at least a little bit. After all, who says, "I am so grateful for all my blessings, tough luck for others"? No sincerely grateful person says that.

Elvis Presley, the king of rock 'n' roll, gave away Cadillacs—a lot of them. To his mother. His employees. A bank teller. A hairdresser. Policemen. Firemen. A TV weatherman. Even complete strangers. He loved how giving Cadillacs to *others* made *him* feel. All smiles! He couldn't stop. He gave away Cadillacs until two weeks before his death. There is even a movie called *200 Cadillacs* documenting his generosity.

Elvis has left the building, so what about the rest of us? What if our life sucks and we *think* we have nothing to be grateful for? How can we serve others when we have so many needs ourselves? That was the question John Kralik tackled in his best-selling book *A Simple Act of Gratitude*. He was a beaten man: twice divorced, distant from his children, and living alone in a run-down apartment. After thirty years as an attorney, he had no savings and bleak prospects. His small law practice was losing money, about to lose its lease, and on the verge of bankruptcy. He was desperate and described his situation as a "tour de force of failure."[108]

How did he turn it around? He chose to find gratitude in his challenging circumstances and proceeded to write 365 "thank-you" notes (actual paper notes, not emails) the following year. Every day he tried to find some human interaction to be thankful for and send that person a note. He sent notes to family members, clients who paid on time, the barista, his building manager, courtroom clerks, you name it. He was up to 720 thank-you notes when his book was published and had countless stories of how those notes changed his relationships with the recipients.

Was he serving others by sending thank-you notes, or thanking others for serving him? For anyone who craves appreciation (which is all of us), Kralik's thank-you notes were their own form of serving others. How many people got his thank-you notes, felt appreciated, and rededicated themselves to doing a good job because someone noticed? It is a virtuous cycle. And who was transformed by finding and expressing gratitude for simple acts of kindness: the person sending or receiving the notes? The answer is "yes."

The moral of the story is that regardless of where we are on the success curve—be it Elvis or a struggling Los Angeles attorney—gratitude is always possible. And where there is a grateful heart, there is a desire to serve others.

So how do we teach our children (and ourselves) to have grateful hearts?

On a secular level, the best we can probably do is to show them overwhelming evidence of their privilege so that they have no reasonable choice but to be grateful for their circumstances and their hearts ache to serve and improve lots of others. How do we do that? By removing them from their comfortable bubbles so that they can see and *experience* how the rest of the world lives. We all need a dose of perspective to appreciate how good we have it as a catalyst to return some of our earned good fortune to our fellow man. Enter the international mission trip.

Unlike a generation ago, the international mission trip is not out of reach for many youngsters. Today, many churches and schools offer "mission" or "humanitarian" trips all over the world. The kids send out "support letters," get the funding, and off they go to Central or South America (Guatemala seems to be a popular choice), or India, or any non-Western country. Once there, not much talking is required. Begging. Pickpockets. Dirty water. Dirty streets. Poor housing. Poor education. Poor sanitation. No fashion designers. No makeup and teenage lifestyle social-media influencers. No Kardashians. No jobs. No futures. The grinding poverty and misery on full display. Only the most cynical teenager (or parent) comes away being unaffected. If honest, most of us return home thinking, *Better them than us.* It's impossible to be ungrateful by comparison. Does this experiential gratitude stick and translate into a desire to serve others, or is it a passing phase?

Sometimes it does stick, absolutely. Some of our kids come back with a newly changed grateful heart and the fruit therefrom is their enduring desire to serve others. And they do. Yet, for the large majority, the hometown experiences resume and overwhelm the mission trip experiences. The grateful heart in Guatemala returns to the status-quo heart at home, and the service to others dwindles and returns to its prior baseline of mandatory volunteerism. But the experience is still there and may later contribute to developing a grateful heart. Having a grateful heart lends itself to serving others. The challenge is to keep it.

The third tool is the reinforcing power of *joy.* When we help others, our own spirits are lifted and moods brightened. It gives direction and purpose to our lives. Elvis felt great giving away Cadillacs. We all feel better when we serve others. It confirms our usefulness to the community and builds our self-esteem, at least a little. Maybe we don't feel like Superman by cutting our sick neighbor's lawn, but we'll feel good when we get the thank-you note. Once the joy and significance of helping others is experienced, it's hard to go back to the shallowness of self on a full-time basis.

Finally, we must serve others NOW, meaning today, and not lose the reinforcing good feeling in doing so. As Kralik's thank-you notes show, we can find small, simple ways to serve others each day. Pretty soon, small acts of service become a daily habit. If we skip days, we forget the good feeling and revert back to our selfish ways. Serving others is like a muscle. We must exercise it daily or it will atrophy.

One last thought when it comes to serving others with money. If led to write a check, do it immediately. If you wait, it will take less than ten minutes to convince yourself of all the reasons not to do it.

In summary, let's give away some Cadillacs (metaphorically speaking, of course).

• MEGGIE'S TAKE •

Ugh, the international mission trip. I knew this was going to come up at some point. Here's the thing. We all go on international mission trips thinking we are doing so much good for a community, and making lives better, and bringing the life-transforming power of the gospel, and rebuilding houses, and hugging babies, and bringing hungry people food, and painting stuff, and giving people medicine. And if we get a couple of social media pictures out of it, surely we deserve that for our efforts, right?

I'm not saying that all mission trips are bad and that missionaries are just trying to curate their social media profile. But even the way Dad is talking about the mission trip here is indicative of how it so often goes, in my opinion. He's trying to convince you to take a mission trip so that you can see your own privilege. And you probably will. But do you see how that is focused on yourself? I know he's trying to give practical tips on how to get into serving more. And it's true, helping others can feel pretty good. But is that why we should be doing it?

This gets into a much deeper question: If you do something good for the wrong reasons or with the wrong motivation, is it still good? And, perhaps more importantly, is the "good" thing you are doing actually good? Ask yourself those questions before you embark on your next mission trip.

Grade: C

DAD ACCOUNTABILITY HOMEWORK

                                                      Answer and Date

1. Dad, how have you modeled service this week?   _____
2. Is this service a regular event or a one-off?   _____
3. For dads wanting to go big on this deposit, continue. _____

DAD ACCOUNTABILITY HOMEWORK: EXTRA CREDIT

                                                      Answer and Date

1. Go on a mission trip with your child.   _____
2. Have discussions on possible locations.   _____
3. Child picks the mission trip.   _____
4. You and child go and serve.   _____
5. Where did you go?   _____
6. Was it a bust or impactful?   _____
7. Will you go back and serve?   _____
8. Grade the experience.   _____

If you feel so led, please join The Super Dad Myth Facebook community group and post your story (and a fun picture!) as inspiration for the next dad.

31. RESPECT THE FUTURE (BUCKET #4)

BUCKET FILLING

Deposit #9   Proclaim the "Success Sequence"
___

Deposit #10 Endure "The Sex Talk"
___

The future does not belong to us; it belongs to our children. There are six generations in America:

1. GI Generation (born in 1924 or earlier)
2. Silent Generation (born 1925–1942)
3. Baby Boomers (born 1943–1964)
4. Generation X (born 1965–1979)
5. Millennials (born 1980–2000)
6. Generation Z (born after 2001)

For those of us in one of the first three generations, we are an ever-growing minority, amounting to only 32 percent of the total population and shrinking. The last two generations already make up nearly 50 percent of the population and growing. The upshot: Each generation gets a short window of time to influence the next generation. And each individual parent gets a very short window of time to influence their children. We need to prepare and equip our children before our generational window slams shut.

Respect that!

32. PROCLAIM THE "SUCCESS SEQUENCE" (DEPOSIT #9)

Proper life sequencing harkens back to Old Testament days with King Solomon in Ecclesiastes 3:1–7 (KJV):

> To everything there is a season, and a time to every purpose under the heaven:
> A time to be born, and a time to die; a time to plant, and a time to pluck up that which is planted;
> A time to kill, and a time to heal; a time to break down, and a time to build up;
> A time to weep, and a time to laugh; a time to mourn, and a time to dance;
> A time to cast away stones, and a time to gather stones together; a time to embrace, and a time to refrain from embracing;
> A time to get, and a time to lose; a time to keep, and a time to cast away;
> A time to rend, and a time to sew; a time to keep silence, and a time to speak

We have been debating proper life sequencing as the secret to success ever since.

Where King Solomon left off, the social scientists and think tanks step in to test life sequencing in the modern age, with Millennials as their research guinea pigs. The term "success sequence" was coined by Brookings Institution scholars Ron Haskins and Isabel Sawhill, and involves three steps: (1) getting at least a high school education, (2) working full time, and (3) getting married before having children—*in that order, no deviation*.[109] Does following the success sequence generally lead to a better life by avoiding poverty? Absolutely. Let's review the data.

According to sociologists Wendy Wang and W. Bradford Wilcox, Millennials who failed all three steps were universally poor, almost without exception. The poverty rate dropped to 31 percent for Millennials who completed high school (Step 1), to 16 percent for those who completed high school and had a full-time job (Steps 1 and 2), and plummeted to 3 percent for those who stayed on track for all three steps of the success sequence.[110] In summary, for Millennials who followed the three-step success sequence track, 97 percent avoided poverty.

Is this really a surprise, or does the research just back up what our parents and grandparents have been preaching for years? "Finish your education so you can get a good job." "Finish school before getting married."

As researcher Wang recounted to the *Wall Street Journal*, in her Chinese hometown no one was taught to wait to have children until marriage.[111] No one *had* to teach it. It simply wasn't done. Is there really any debate here? Does anyone really believe the path to prosperity is to drop out of high school and have out-of-wedlock children? Haven't we all heard this before?

Apparently not. According to Brookings Institution scholar Richard Reeves, as chronicled in the *Wall Street Journal*, the "success sequence" message breaks down along economic lines. Reeves has even argued that the success sequence is being "hoarded" by the American upper class to the exclusion of the poor.[112] That smacks of rhetorical exaggeration, but the disparity in applying the message to Millennials remains.

The cure? Let's proclaim the time-honored "success sequence" to our children and all who will listen. And let's show them the data. For those who follow the success sequence, there is a 97 percent chance they will not live in poverty. For those who fail to follow the success sequence, there is a nearly 100 percent chance they will live in poverty.

Just like Grandma used to say.

• MEGGIE'S TAKE •

I mean, this is research, so it can't possibly be wrong, right? The sequence makes sense to me as the optimal way to do things, and I think it's definitely fair for parents to encourage their kids to follow this timetable. We kids are sometimes dumb, though, so I think it might also be a good idea to have a discussion about what would happen if one of the steps didn't occur, or happened in the wrong order. The point of that discussion isn't to scare your kids into doing the right thing, because remember, we all think we're invincible and nothing bad will happen to us. Instead, I think it would be a good time to calmly discuss what your kid would do if he found himself in the nonoptimal situation of not following the steps correctly.

As soon as you make your kid take ownership of an issue, it changes the issue completely. Move the discussion from "You're going to ruin your life if you do X" toward "You don't want to finish high school? Come back to me with a list of jobs you'd be able to get with their associated salaries, and I'll show you exactly how much money it takes for you to live your current lifestyle."

It's hard to scare someone who feels invincible, but lucky for you, it's also hard for a kid to argue with something he actually investigated himself.

Grade: A

DAD ACCOUNTABILITY HOMEWORK

	Check One	
	Yes	No

1. Can your child state the three-step success sequence a week later? _____ _____
   If not, repeat until the answer is yes.

33. ENDURE "THE SEX TALK" (DEPOSIT #10)

The third step of the success sequence requires getting married before having children. This requires having the sex talk with our teenagers.

This is brutal, but necessary. What father looks forward to talking with his son or daughter about puberty, the mechanics of sex, STDs, HIV, or the consequences of an unplanned teen pregnancy? Flip it: What son or daughter wants to talk about sex with his or her parents? Awkward all around! Can't we just leave it to the high school health class, where maybe abstinence will be mentioned? Can't we just avoid the whole subject and hope it all works out? Maybe, but Bristol Palin says hello.

Fathers, we can't dodge this one—unless we want our basement converted into the new "bedroom suite" for our teenage daughter, new grandchild, and on-again, off-again boyfriend. No, thanks! We must fight for our children's futures and encourage them to wait until they are self-sufficient, married adults before having children to care for. We need to have these discussions or risk hearing those dreaded words: "It just happened," or "We love each other." NOT ON OUR WATCH! Tell your teenager it's time to talk . . . NOW!

But how do we go about having the sex talk? Step #1: Pass our daughters off to their mothers (or grandmothers). They are fully equipped to have the woman-to-teenage-girl sex talk. Done. That leaves just the boys. One thing is for sure, we don't go it alone. We don't wing it. We don't reinvent the wheel. No, we get our hands on a solid resource and then follow the script.

Depending on your worldview, we recommend the following resources to navigate the sex talk with your teenager.

Worldview	Resource
Spiritual	*Passport2Purity* by Dennis and Barbara Rainey, Family Life
	Preparing Your Son for Every Man's Battle by Stephen Arterburn and Fred Stoeker
Secular	"Choosing the Best," a sex-education curriculum used throughout the state of Georgia. The more permissive "Flash Curriculum" is a sex-education program used throughout the state of Washington.

If we do nothing? Statistically, 95 percent of our teenagers will dodge pregnancy. The teen pregnancy rate (including live births, abortions, or miscarriages) for women aged 15–19 years old was 43.4 per 1,000 women in 2013 (the most recent data available), according to the Department of Health and Human Services.[113]

And for the 5 percent of teenagers who do get pregnant with our grandchildren in tow? Then we're back to the parental starting line, this time helping our children raise our grandchildren. We must love them and support them (emotionally and financially), because otherwise they are headed toward a hardscrabble life of poverty and dependence. Perhaps it would be better to have the talk instead.

DAD ACCOUNTABILITY HOMEWORK

	Check One	
	Yes	No
1. Did you endure the "sex talk"?	_____	_____
2. Did you build the basement bedroom suite?	_____	_____

You have to do one or the other. Your choice.

34. DON'T QUIT

We all have to decide when to hang it up and stop filling the buckets with parental deposits. We all get old, but some try to be a "young/old" dad and not an "old/old" dad for as long as possible. Some dads get the kids out of the house and rapidly disappear from the scene. Others never quit and are carried off the parental battlefield on their shields. The choice is always the same, whether at the beginning or end of the journey: Stay active, or pack it in?

We can adapt to the changing world shaped by the next generation, or quit, disengage, and live in the comfortable world of our past. As our children age, the latter sounds tempting; after all, we don't want to "meddle" or "interfere" in the lives of our adult children, do we? Yet isn't the better course to find the right balance of appropriate engagement without crossing over into meddlesome-dad territory?

Perhaps nowhere is this quit-or-don't-quit dilemma more apparent than in what our kids talk about and the ways they now communicate.

Confronting the Social Media Beast

The world of social media is never going away. Never. Unfortunately, our children live on their phones and in front of their screens. Technology is relentless and a major driver for whether our children live stable and productive lives, but that is the subject of an entirely different book.

What is our response to this strange new world? Do we run onto the social-media field and mix it up, or quit and surrender this field to the younger set? Let's tackle this generational divide and plot our attack forward, casting aside any thoughts of quitting or retreat.

"I don't do social media. It's just a time-wasting, privacy-invading bunch of nonsense" is a common refrain by many of us out-of-touch fathers (who apparently wish to remain so). It is even said with a ring of old-school pride. TikTok? Snapchat? Twitter? Forget about it, never heard of 'em! That attitude will work for about 10 percent of us. According to University of North Carolina researcher Jacqueline Nesi, around 10 percent of teenagers abstain from social-media use.[114] So, if all of your children run in the minority non–social media users pack, then you're fine. Relax and skip forward to the next section. However, for the rest of us, we must try to tame this social media beast that is devouring our children. Start by finding out and limiting their daily "screen time" to a reasonable number -- opinions vary. (I'm ashamed to say, for 15 years and older, we permit 2 hours on weekdays, 3 hours on weekends). If you don't know their screen time usage, you are a dinosaur, way behind and will likely be shocked when you see the numbers. Prepare yourselves. The statistics are scary.

A 2015 survey from the Pew Research Center reported by the *Wall Street Journal* found that 92 percent of teenagers (ages thirteen through seventeen) go online daily, including 24 percent who say they are on their devices "almost constantly." According to an April 2016 survey from the Piper Jaffray Company, Snapchat is the teenager's social-media platform of choice, with 28 percent of teenagers voting for it, followed by Instagram at 27 percent.[115] An amazing 67 percent of American kids between the ages of eighteen and twenty-four communicate through Snapchat daily.[116] A recent Gallup nationwide survey found that the average US teenager spends 5 hours on social media platforms daily, far exceeding the time spent either on daily homework or classroom instruction. It is the most dominate activity in their days, except for sleeping. Sadly, every day our children average 4.5 more hours on social media than with us. The time totals at the end of each week: Social media: 35 hours; Dad-child: 3.5 hours. A factor of 10X. We are losing our teenagers to social media and need to either surrender or get in the social media fight.

How can we effectively communicate with our teenagers if we don't speak the same language? What are we telling our teenagers by thinking so little of their forms of communication that we ignore, or even mock, social media? Sadly, the failure to engage in social media (or even texting) oftentimes hides a much larger failing: We choose to have *nothing meaningful to say*. It is much easier to use the "I don't do social media" excuse than admit we really prefer to pursue our own personal interests and not invest the time and energy required to have meaningful communication with our teenagers.

Social Media Is Doable

Take a look around. There are very successful adults from every profession and walk of life who claim to be completely befuddled by social media: the mechanic who puts together complicated engines, the doctor who makes life-and-death decisions involving complex pathologies, the pastor who ministers to his flock, or the teacher who keeps thirty children in check while teaching geometry. Every job has its unique difficulties and complications that are solved every day, but social media is the unsolvable? Now that is nonsense!

By the way, many of us who use the "I don't do social media" excuse aren't exactly putting pen to paper and cranking out good old-fashioned letters. Take this test. When was the last time you wrote a meaningful letter to your child? This month? This year? Last year? Hmm, maybe social media isn't the problem, after all. But more on that later.

There's good news. Social media is an area where fathers are graded on a huge curve. This is the rare area in life where our kids will (secretly) give us an "A for effort," despite our turning out a barely passable product. In fact, teenagers are utterly amazed by even our attempts to speak their social-media language.

"It's kind of shocking," said Paris Zeikos, an eighteen-year-old university student in Manchester, England. "Most people who use Snapchat are in my generation, so it's bizarre to see someone older use Snapchat."[117]

Mr. Zeikos said it all. A father's use of Snapchat is nothing short of shocking—some might even say bizarre—to the younger set. The statistics back up Mr. Zeikos, as only 14 percent of adults over thirty-five years old have the Snapchat app. Fewer actually use it.[118] As aging fathers, we should welcome our social-media skills being described as shocking or bizarre. That sure beats the usual description of being clueless, lame, or bewildered when it comes to all things technology.

"Nonsense" is what some are saying right now. Many are not convinced of the need to play the social-media game to effectively communicate with their kids; after all, effective parenting did somehow exist before the invention of social media. Of course, that is right, and we concede the point. A father can certainly convey meaningful and consistent messages without the tool of social media. But it isn't as easy as it used to be.

We know a father who really put the rest of us to shame. For years, he took his children out to breakfast *one-on-one every week* to really find out what was going on in their lives and impart meaningful wisdom tailored to their individual circumstances. Then, together, they created a detailed "life plan" (see prior section) based on certain values to help the child survive and thrive in today's culture. This was all done without social media, was highly effective, and contributed to producing great kids. Good for them! Reality-check time: How many of us will make the time for all that? Most of us can't even manage a *monthly* date night with our spouse, so how are we going to pull off *weekly* one-on-one meals with each kid? We need help!

The reality is that if we just give it a try, social media makes communications with our kids *easier and more frequent*. It permits us to compete against the breakfast-club dads out there. How, exactly? First, we gain insight as to what topics our kids care about by reading (translation: stalking) their posts. Second, we gain insight as to who is in their inner circle (hopefully not news) by seeing who is regularly liking or commenting on their posts. Third, it gives us a break from having to *initiate* the conversation all the time, as they initiate the topics through their posts. This is huge! We all know what it is like to always have to initiate conversation with a teenager. It goes something like this: "So, how was your day at school?" Long pause, look up, look down, sigh, then utter one word: "Fine." Okie dokie, good talk. Some of our teenagers (and we parents) are not the best conversationalists. It's work. Social media allows teenagers to initiate the conversation. Fourth, we can *engage* by commenting on or liking their posts. This is tricky territory, so let's run an example so we don't mess up.

Say your teen posts something online. This is helpful, as we can glean what is important to her by what she's posting, and she is the one *initiating* the conversation. Now comes the challenging part: Do we comment on (or like) her post for all her friends to see, or do we just tuck it away as something to talk about offline at home? A lot of parental rookie mistakes happen right here, as there is a strict, yet unwritten code that must be followed to be in the cool-dad club. Comment too much or on off-limit topics, and we're out. Comment too little, and we're irrelevant.

So, what's the balance? A good rule of thumb is to always comment on family-related or food posts, occasionally comment on sports posts, but never, *ever* comment on (or even like) music, school, or political posts. These are strictly off limits. Finally, and most importantly, we must bring our "A-game" content. Our comments must be funny, playful, positive, or insightful. Save the criticism and corrections for only clearly inappropriate posts, and handle that offline. If we're not sure, then we just "like" it and move on rather than be lame and compromise our social-media currency.

Maybe some of us want to start smaller, not yet ready to join the over one billion Facebook users around the globe (what do they know, anyway?). Besides, all the moms (and even grandmothers) are on Facebook, so how cool can it really be? Even Facebook founder Mark Zuckerberg admitted that as the largest social-media platform on the planet, "Coolness is done for us."[119] No problem; there is always Snapchat or Instagram or the next great app. Social media permits more one-on-one communication, mostly through pictures or videos taken on our smartphones (yes, it's time to retire our trusty flip phones), so get with the program, at least a little bit.

Texting: The Poor Man's Social Media

Still not convinced? Not to worry, there is still one digital option left: *texting*. Surely we can text. We're just pressing buttons on our smartphone! Texting can go a long, long way. It's not the same as social media, but for the late adopters, it is a good intermediary step before the inevitable social-media capitulation. It seems funny now, but back in the 1930s and '40s there were those few old-timers who didn't want a phone in their homes. They were noisy, expensive, and a waste of time, as people just talked and gossiped. Sound familiar? Eventually, everyone had a phone in their home, except now the landlines are going away in favor of smartphones. Eventually, all but the very few will be communicating in the social-media world, so get with the program, old man.

US Postal Service: Snail Mail to the Rescue for All Fathers

At the other end of the social-media spectrum are the nondigital dads. They don't overuse social media. To the contrary, these dads don't use it at all. It's just not in the cards. Not to worry. For the hardcore nondigital fathers, there is hope. Actually, for all fathers there is a very nice attention-getting option to differentiate ourselves from the noisy and busy world of emails, texts, and social-media posts: *letters*. Yes, actual physical letters! You know, the kind with envelopes and stamps that we can actually hold in our hands. It doesn't sound exciting. It doesn't sound sexy. But when done right, we can score major deposits with our children.

Ask your teenager or your college kid this question: "What emails, texts, or social-media posts did you receive today?" You better get comfortable, because the answer is "A lot." Next, ask this question: "What letters or notes did you receive in the mail today?" The typical answer: "None." We can ask our children the same questions tomorrow and get the same answers. They typically never get any meaningful letters. Many young people don't bother checking their mailboxes at all. Why would they? They rarely get mail. Many kids can go their entire high school and college careers (or entire life) and never get a letter or note from their dads in the mail. How sad.

This presents a huge communication opportunity for us. Sending letters and notes to our children is powerful. It means they know we are thinking of them enough to take the time and trouble of putting pen to paper, stuffing an envelope, licking a stamp, and dropping the letter into a mailbox. The content doesn't even have to be that great, as the effort alone goes a long, long way. Here's the best part: We have no competition. None! Almost no one takes the time to write personal letters and notes anymore. We have the field entirely to ourselves. Even if we send only two letters a month, that will be two more letters than they will probably get from anyone else. Also, we can throw in a sincere "I love you" in our notes, which adds to our "say the words" deposits. We didn't just say the words, we put them in *writing*! Talk about extra credit! Show that to the peer group.

One father shared with us that when his daughter went off to college, he knew he could not compete against all her friends and family members in the social-media world, so his goal was to "dominate her college mailbox." It turned out it wasn't hard to do, because despite her being part of a large family, no one else wrote her letters. He would write her, on average, once every couple of weeks. Sometimes more, sometimes less. She went to her mailbox not expecting to get any mail, except from her dad. That is the only reason she even bothered to check. He's the only one who consistently wrote to her. Over time, her college mailbox became a de facto private message box between dad and daughter.

What was he writing? Was there really that much to say to warrant written letters once a week? How did he keep the weekly pace of letters going? He cheated, that's how. Most of it wasn't his content. His daughter was interested in medicine, football, running, and religion. He had sticky notes made with his name on the top. He'd read the daily paper and when he came across an article in one of her areas of interest, he'd cut it out, put his sticky note on it with a brief comment, throw in an "I love you," and mail it out. That was it. That was the majority of his notes and letters, simply passing along the words and ideas *from others*. But that was more than anyone else was doing. Every time she opened her mailbox and got one of those notes, *in that moment* she knew that he was thinking about her and no one else was. Now, repeat that over a four-year college career, and you know he left a mark. He won the mailbox war not because his letters and notes were particularly insightful (they weren't, and many were lame), but because there was no competition. He "dominated" the mailbox.

Final Communication Thoughts

There are many lessons here. Can we be impactful fathers and never touch the social media to which our kids flock? Of course we can, but we must keep communicating in some fashion. Snail mail can work. Phone calls can work. But why not give social media a try? Given how immersed our children are in social media, how long can we ignore it entirely as a method to communicate with our kids? What message does our unwillingness to learn their language communicate to them about their value to us? Maybe nothing, but why ignore social media, since it is easy and leads to more frequent communication with our kids?

Some fathers get it and are playing the long game by creating private "family" social-media accounts for only themselves and immediate family members. Each family member periodically posts pictures, videos, and comments. So, together, they are creating something very special: a lasting family diary that captures many small moments of their childhoods that would otherwise have been forever lost. In future years, these families will experience immeasurable joy from looking back at long-ago pictures, videos, and comments of earlier family days captured by social media. Good for them and their descendants for being early adopters.

Will we master all social-media channels? Of course not, so let's pick one or two (please, no more than two) that work for us. Shoot, even eighty-year-old Pope Francis is on Instagram and Twitter. If he can do it, we can get in the game.

Social media is a tool every dad can use to communicate with his children on their terms. Isn't that the point? What a great gift! We can use this gift or leave it unopened. The choice is entirely ours, but don't pretend the gift is too complicated to open and use.

Will we make mistakes in navigating the social-media world? Yes, but here is the good news: We are off the social-media sidelines and *in the game*. With some practice, we'll soon join that elite group of "bizarre" parents that "shock" our kids with our social-media skills. Take that, breakfast-club dads!

Don't quit!

• MEGGIE'S TAKE •

This section is hilarious. It does sometimes feel like we are speaking a different language from our parents when it comes to social media, and some kids would rather keep it that way. But I've also found social media to be a really fun way to connect with my parents (definitely an "A for effort" situation). It's pretty hilarious to get Snapchat selfies of Mom and Dad every once in a while, or watch Dad try to work with filters or make a Facebook post. For all his big talk, he would have no idea how to work most of Snapchat's features if my sisters and I hadn't helped him, but that's half the fun.

That being said, the section about gaining "insights as to who is in their inner circle by seeing who is regularly liking or commenting on their posts" sounds very stalkerish and pretty terrifying. There are a lot of ways for kids to hide content from their parents on these apps, so I wouldn't recommend thinking you know too much just because you saw one picture your kid posted. This "stalker" approach will probably also backfire by giving your kids more reason to argue that you are too controlling.

Instead, I think social media is best used as a way to relate to your kids, with just a little stalking on the side. Finally, just FYI, Instagram is the latest, Dad. It might be time for you to step up your game.

Grade: A (for effort)

• CHAPTER 5 •

THE RECONCILING DAD: VERTICAL RECONCILIATION (CHILD-TO-GOD)

Vertical Reconciliation

God

Child

To recap, in Chapters 1–3, we presented celebrities doing stupid stuff that our children should avoid. In Chapter 4, we presented ten deposits into four secular buckets.

Affirm the Child (Bucket #1)

Deposit #1.	Do It: The Deeds
Deposit #2.	Run Away with Your Child: Take One Memorable Trip
Deposit #3.	Have That "One Thing" with Your Kid
Deposit #4.	Say It! The Three Most Powerful Words
Deposit #5.	Affirmation > Correction 10:1 Ratio

Love the Mother (Bucket #2)

Deposit #6.   Leave Your Crown in the Garage
Deposit #7.   Honor and Respect Your Children's Mother

Serve Others (Bucket #3)

Deposit #8.   Serve Others Today

Respect the Future (Bucket #4)

Deposit #9.   Proclaim the "Success Sequence"
Deposit #10.   Endure "The Sex Talk"

Chapters 1–4 were intended to accomplish two goals: (1) to reconcile ourselves to our child (horizontal reconciliation), increasing our chances of being effective messengers to them, and (2) to present an effective secular message pointing them in the direction of a stable, decent life.

If that is all we're looking to accomplish—a good relationship with our child, who is, in turn, experiencing a stable life—then we're pretty much done here. But before closing it out, consider something far better than mere horizontal reconciliation (i.e. child-to-parent). Consider *vertical reconciliation*: reconciling our children to God, if you believe in that sort of thing.

Why is vertical reconciliation better than horizontal reconciliation? Read on.

35. TWO FATHERS, TWO INHERITANCES

There are two categories of inheritance: earthly and eternal. If a child enjoys horizontal reconciliation—i.e. child reconciled to parent—then he or she will likely be the beneficiary of a secular inheritance bequeathed by a deceased parent, which is nice for the recipient. On the other hand, if there is no horizontal reconciliation—i.e. a divisive parent-child relationship—the parent may well cut the child out of his will. It happens. A large financial inheritance can certainly provide earthly assurance, but only for a season before being consumed or passed to the next generation to be consumed. Even great wealth is fleeting, as "ninety percent of families squander their wealth by the third generation."[120]

Now, if the child enjoys vertical reconciliation—i.e. child reconciled to God—then he or she is the beneficiary of a spiritual inheritance for a better earthly life (albeit not necessarily a better lifestyle) and eternal life later. More on that in Part II.

Which child has received the richer inheritance: the child that is cash rich/God poor (secular: horizontal reconciliation) or the child that is cash poor/God rich (spiritual: vertical reconciliation)? Which do we want for our children? Which inheritance will last and pass from one generation to the next?

The bottom line is that Chapters 1–4 were designed to accomplish something hard: horizontal reconciliation with our children. *We've reconciled our children to ourselves: child-to-parent.* In other words, we've built a solid relationship with them. We've earned an audience with them. They may listen, consider, and maybe even adopt our message promoting a stable life.

But the $64,000 question is, what message are we going to point them to: a secular, limited message (Part I) or a spiritual, limitless message (Part II)?

Horizontal reconciliation is great; *reconciling our children to ourselves* probably leads to a satisfying, lifelong parental-child relationship. But if we only point them to man's ways (secular message), the upside is limited. The best outcome? Living a stable and productive life, the duration of which is one lifetime.

Vertical reconciliation means so much more because we are *reconciling our children to God.* Why not point them to God's ways (spiritual message) with a limitless upside? The best outcome: a better life now and eternal life later.

Which is better? Horizontal reconciliation (child-to-parent) with a secular, temporary message, or vertical reconciliation (child-to-God) with a spiritual, eternal message?

Horizontal Reconciliation Only

Child ⟶ Parent

or

Horizontal and Vertical Reconciliation

God (Vertical Reconciliation)

↑

Parent ⟶ Child (Horizontal Reconciliation)

36. JOURNEY'S END FOR THE DISAPPEARING DAD

Decision time. Who will our children *follow*: the Disappearing Dad—us (Part I)—or the Forever Father—God (Part II)? Is horizontal reconciliation enough, or will we go for vertical reconciliation? What *path* will we point our children toward: the wide, secular path, or the narrow, spiritual path? For those who chose to follow the Disappearing Dad on the secular path (Part I), this is the end of the book. It is time to answer the "Final Question" posed at the beginning—namely, who is your child's permanent father? For Part I readers, the answer is YOU, the Disappearing Dad. Your positive paternal legacy will last about fifty years. After that, the advance (or decline) of your descendants is in the hands of people you will never know (and who won't know you). Your name, influence, and earthly inheritance will be completely lost to family history. Yet what can we do? We rest comfortably in the knowledge that we took our generational turn at the head table, moved the biological marker forward, and fought the good fight. The baton has been passed. We did all we could *humanly* do while under the sun.

Please proceed to the Life Verdict Form at the end of the book, mark "Disappearing Dad (Man)," and sign your verdict.

Thank you for taking this journey.

THE END FOR PART I READERS

A PREVIEW FOR PART II:
OPENING THE DOOR TO A SPIRITUAL LIFE

Here I am! I stand at the door and knock. If anyone hears my voice and opens the door, I will come in and eat with that person, and they with me.

—Revelation 3:20

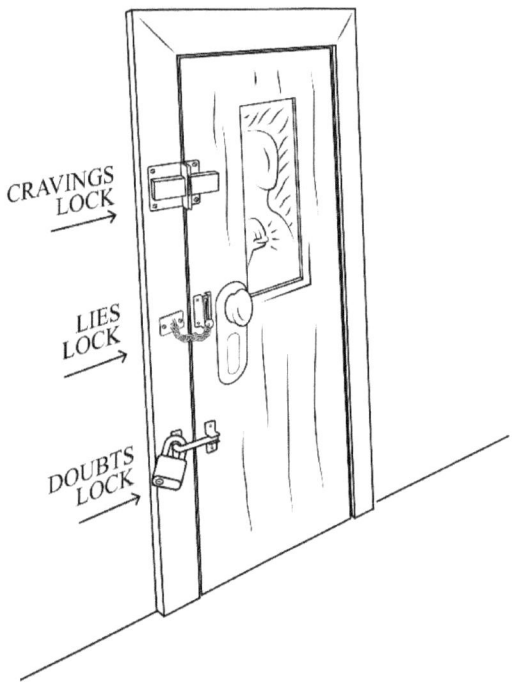

Let's revisit vertical reconciliation: reconciling our children to God. It's a simple concept: Open the door to a spiritual life and *follow the Forever Father (God)* in the conduct of our lives and in raising our children. By pointing to God and following Him, it will improve our earthly life (but not necessarily lifestyle) and ensure our eternal one. That is the secret weapon to life and parenting the lives of others. We call it Bucket #5 and Deposit #11. But many locks keep the spiritual door closed for most.

37. WORSHIP THE KING (BUCKET #5)

BUCKET FILLING

Deposit #11   Believe in and Follow the Forever Father

Who says we need the parental help? For fathers who have it all figured out, then agreed—go it alone. That is what Part I (a secular viewpoint) is all about. It can be done. It's done all the time. No judgment.

But for fathers who believe that God's wisdom may be worth considering, doesn't it make sense to use such wisdom, particularly if it reinforces our own beliefs? Biblical wisdom may be the secret weapon in parenting our children. But how would that work? Simple. God left behind a life instruction manual called the Bible that provides answers to our struggles and dilemmas. For any question or dilemma that comes up, we simply say to our teenager, "What does the Bible say about that?" If it answers the question, then we're off the hook and can merely reinforce the existing answer. Why reinvent the wheel? Does it make sense to exclude God's wisdom simply because it came from the Bible? Wisdom is wisdom.

The beauty of this approach is that (1) we don't have to figure out the answers, as they are already written down, and (2) we don't have to justify our gut-instinct answers with the old standby rationale "because I said so." (Our kids really love that one.) The answers and wisdom are from Almighty God, so who are we to quibble? If our teenagers choose to ignore such wisdom, so be it. But they aren't resisting us; they are resisting God's wisdom.

38. PARENTAL SECRET WEAPON: CO-PARENTING WITH THE FOREVER FATHER

Let's completely suspend reality and imagine how it might work if we were to partner with the Forever Father on difficult coming-of-age teenager issues.

On Premarital Sex

Child: "Now that I'm eighteen, have a steady boyfriend, and am thinking more for myself, I've done some research on premarital sex. The CDC says 88 percent of women between the ages of fifteen and forty-four have had premarital sex.[121] Did you know that, Dad?"

Dad: "Umm . . . who's this fella again?"

Child: "And did you know that same study showed that 89 percent of men had premarital sex?"

Dad: "Umm . . . exactly how long have you been dating this guy, and *why* are we talking about a boyfriend in the context of premarital sex?"

Child: "Now, Dad, if 88 percent of women and 89 percent of men have premarital sex, do you agree that premarital sex is now culturally acceptable?"

Dad: "Well, what does the manual say about the acceptability of premarital sex?"

Child: "Come on, Dad. You really expect me to go to the Bible for guidance on premarital sex?"

Dad: "Do you really think my advice would be better than that of the Bible?"

Child: "Good point. You're as clueless about how things work in today's world as the Babylonians of Old Testament times."

Dad: "Thanks . . . I think. Anyway, in looking at the manual, I see that it says in Hebrews 13:4 (ESV), 'Let marriage be held in honor among all, and let the marriage bed be undefiled, for God will judge the sexually immoral and adulterous.' It also says in 1 Corinthians 7:2, 'But since sexual immorality is occurring, each man should have sexual relations with his own wife, and each woman with her own husband.' The manual seems clear on this one. Any other questions?"

On Underage Drinking

Child: "I know the legal drinking age is twenty-one, but now that I'm a high school senior, everyone drinks at parties. Also, I'll be going to college in the fall, where absolutely everyone will be drinking! Certainly you don't expect me to not drink in college, do you?"

Dad: "Well, I have my thoughts, but you know where to begin to answer that question, right?"

Child: "Let me guess—the manual. Are you going to dodge all my questions by pointing me to the Bible first?"

Dad: "Pretty much, unless you think I can provide better answers than God."

Child: "Again, fair point. Actually, I did check the Bible and found solid biblical support permitting me to drink in college, provided it is in moderation."

Dad: "Oh, really? You found biblical support for underage drinking?"

Child: "Sure did. In Ecclesiastes 9:7 it is written, 'Go, eat your food with gladness, and drink your wine with a joyful heart, for God has already approved what you do.' And in Ephesians 5:18 it says, 'Do not get drunk on wine, which leads to debauchery. Instead, be filled with the Spirit.' You see, Dad? There is no mention of a legal age. The only point is to drink in moderation and not get drunk."

Dad:	"Yes, I see your point about drinking in moderation, but are you sure that underage drinking is permitted in the Bible?"
Child:	"Dad, I checked, and there is no drinking age specified anywhere in the Bible."
Dad:	"True, but in Romans 13:1–2 it is written, 'Let everyone be subject to the governing authorities, for there is no authority except that which God has established. The authorities that exist have been established by God. Consequently, whoever rebels against the authority is rebelling against what God has instituted, and those who do so will bring judgment on themselves.' The governing authorities of our state require a person to be twenty-one to legally drink alcohol, and God requires that we follow the governing authorities. You see where I'm heading with this . . ."
Child:	"Unfortunately, yes."
Dad:	"It seems the manual is clear on that. Any other questions?"
Child:	"No, you'd probably only tell me to check the manual, anyway!"

As dads, why would we want to figure out all the parental rules on our own when we can access a treasure trove of helpful material? Of course, our children will not always obey the rules, regardless of their source authority. However, invoking a higher authority is better than making up half-baked rules on the fly.

What about fathers who don't believe in God or Jesus? What about those who are only *investigating* the claims of Christ, or who have no interest at all? Easy. Still use the wisdom from the Bible as you see fit. Where you agree with what the Bible says, use it. Where you don't, ignore it. Plenty of thoughtful people disbelieved the divinity of Christ, including Thomas Jefferson and James Madison, but still embraced the wisdom of the Bible. If biblical wisdom was useful to our founding fathers in forming the nation, wouldn't it be hubris to ignore such wisdom in forming our own households? If the Bible is not for you, then find your own secular source as an aid for parental decision-making.

We're not Super Dads. We all need help. Don't go it alone.

39. PARENTAL SECRET WEAPON SUMMARY

Remember, we're all dead men walking. In fifty years, the inheritance money will be long gone. So hopefully we leave behind something more meaningful, i.e. the secret weapon. Again, the secret weapon is to believe in and follow the Forever Father in the conduct of our lives, and we do that by pointing our children to a messenger (Jesus Christ) and message (gospel) to give lasting satisfaction and purpose to their lives.

Are you curious about what a spiritual life or God-focused life might look like? Do you sense something missing from your day-to-day life? Is the culture way ahead of you in influencing your child, and you have no ready response? If you answered yes to any of these questions, we encourage you to read on.

On the other hand, if you have figured out and nailed life's satisfaction and purpose questions, then terrific. If your child is influenced by you rather than the dominating culture and is already on the stable and productive citizen path, then great. Stop here. But if you are at all curious, we encourage you to continue your personal faith investigation by reading Part II. What's the harm? We promise Part II isn't boring as we identify three locks that keep folks from opening the door to a spiritual life. If you are not convinced, so be it.

Know that Part II provides a *totally different* answer to the final question of who your child's permanent father is. Part II changes everything. Some dads may proceed to Part II with zero intention of seeking any heart or life change for themselves, but seek it for their children, so they read on. If that is your intention, be careful—you are playing with fire. The message you seek to influence and convict your child with may collect your heart also. You have been warned (or promised)!

• PART II •

FOLLOW HIM: THE FOREVER FATHER ABOVE THE SUN

For those who have gotten this far, it was not the celebrity stories that got you here. You could have easily stopped at the end of Part I. God has you thinking about your larger purpose. God has you curious about the eternal. God is doing regenerative work in your heart. Simply put, God is at work in you.

You feel God stirring your heart. You feel a nudge to change your worldview from the temporal (man) to the Eternal (God). God has called you to respond, but how? Join us as we break open the three locks that keep us from answering God's knock at the door.

• CHAPTER 6 •

THE CRAVINGS LOCK

"Just a little bit more," John D. Rockefeller replied.

Rockefeller was the wealthiest man in American history. In 1870, he founded Standard Oil and would eventually control 90 percent of the oil business. He was the first man to be worth more than $1 billion. In 1937, his fortune was the equivalent of "nearly 2 percent of *total* U.S. economic output" as measured by gross domestic product (GDP).[122] For perspective, in 2017, the US economy was $19 trillion by GDP. Doing the math, 2 percent of $19 trillion is $380 billion. Jeff Bezos, founder of Amazon, was the richest man in 2017, with a fortune topping $100 billion (before the later divorce). Hard to believe, but Rockefeller was three times richer than Bezos as measured relative to the percentage of national GDP.

Back to his quote above. A reporter once asked Rockefeller, "How much money is enough?"

Rockefeller replied, "Just a little bit more."[123]

His response says it all. He amassed financial success greater than any person in history. He had asymmetric control over American life, possessing whatever he wanted. But it wasn't enough.

40. ENOUGH IS NEVER ENOUGH TO SATISFY

This craving for more isn't unique to Rockefeller; it's part of the human psyche. To illustrate, America presents a case study for the "enough is never enough to satisfy" concept. Over the past two hundred years, American prosperity has exploded upward by any objective metric—life expectancy, health, education, or wealth.

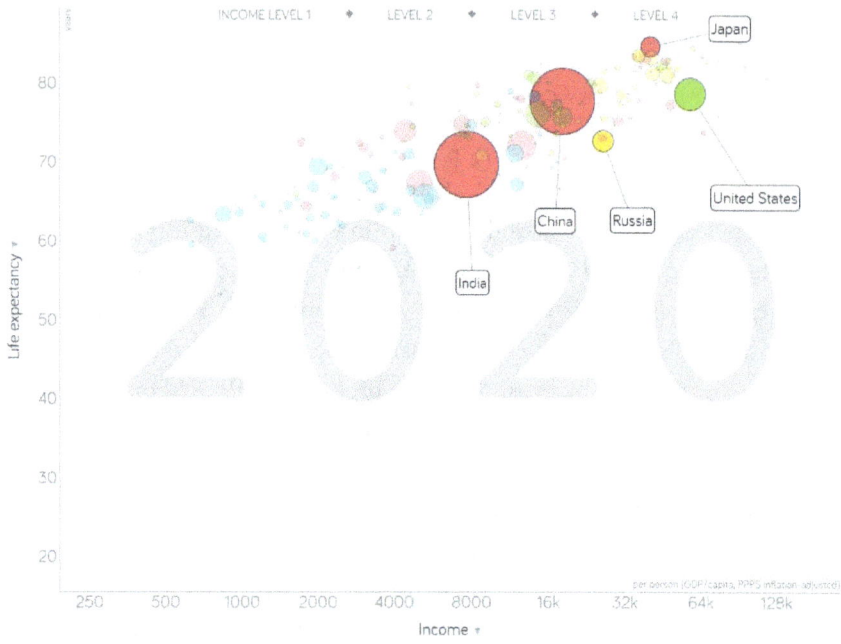

From Gapminder.org[124]

The average American in 1800 had a life expectancy of 39.4 years and an annual income of $1,970. The average American in 2020 has a life expectancy of 78.6 years and annual income of $57,500 (in constant dollars) – increases of 99% and 2,818%, respectively. Amazing!

Whether individually (Rockefeller) or as a society (America), we enjoy more success and progress by nearly every measure than every other major group in the *history of the world*.

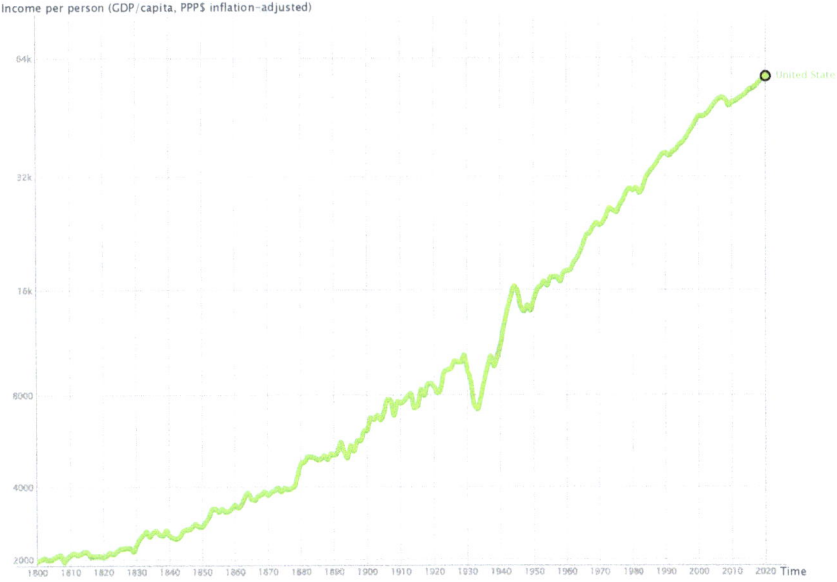

From Gapminder.org[125]

Are we satisfied? Not really. Peggy Noonan, Ronald Reagan's speechwriter and Pulitzer Prize-winning author, bluntly called our never-ending success cravings a "sickness." She explained, "But there is something sick about America that no matter how much success you have, it's not enough, you must have more. And everyone must know you have it."[126]

Noonan is wrong. Cravings are not an American sickness; it is a human condition infecting all peoples. All of humanity suffers from cravings and its ugly side effects of division and envy. This begs the questions, what is the cause of our cravings sickness, is there a cure, and if so, do we want it?

41. THE CAUSE OF CRAVINGS

The cause of cravings? Simple—*man's nature*. Alone, we can't help ourselves. As Paul explained in Ephesians 2:3, "All of us also lived among them at one time, gratifying the cravings of our flesh and following its desires and thoughts."

Is there a cure to change our nature and curb our pointless cravings of the flesh? Yes. But if we accept the cure, must we give up our cravings? Yes. But the good news is that if we accept the cure, our old cravings will fall away and be replaced by new desires of the heart. With help, we have the ability to break away from our earthly cravings for something and someone better. Let's simplify.

There are three basic worldviews regarding the nature of man: Moral Man, Natural Man, and Spiritual Man.

The Moral Man

The Moral Man has one nature: the mind and body bound as one in goodness (selflessness). The Moral Man is basically good (i.e. selfless). He may have some selfish or destructive impulses, but through willpower, he overcomes these bad impulses most of the time and lives as a good person doing good deeds. As a good person who has lived a good life, he has earned his way to eternal life. After all, a loving God would not bar a good person who did good deeds from heaven. There is no particular need for a savior, since access to heaven is based on doing good deeds, not on a belief in a messiah. Most people prefer this Moral Man worldview. Why? Because most people view themselves as good, not bad. The Moral Man worldview is very popular and has a wide path for its many followers.

The Natural Man

The Natural Man also has one nature: the mind and body bound as one in sin (selfishness). The Natural Man is born into sin and is bad (i.e. selfish). Alone, he cannot overcome his selfish or destructive impulses and will live out his one nature as a selfish person who does selfish deeds. He may appear to do some good deeds on the surface, but the motivation behind the good deeds remains selfish, not sacrificial. This Natural Man worldview is rejected by most people. Why? Again, because most people view themselves as good, not bad.

The Spiritual Man

The Spiritual Man has two competing natures: (1) the mind renewed and (2) the body (flesh) not renewed. The Spiritual Man starts out just like the Natural Man, born into sin with one nature: body and mind bound together in sin. By accepting Jesus Christ into his heart through faith (being "born again"), the Natural Man is justified, becoming a "new creation"[127]; hence, a Spiritual Man. The Natural Man and Spiritual Man are depicted on the following page.

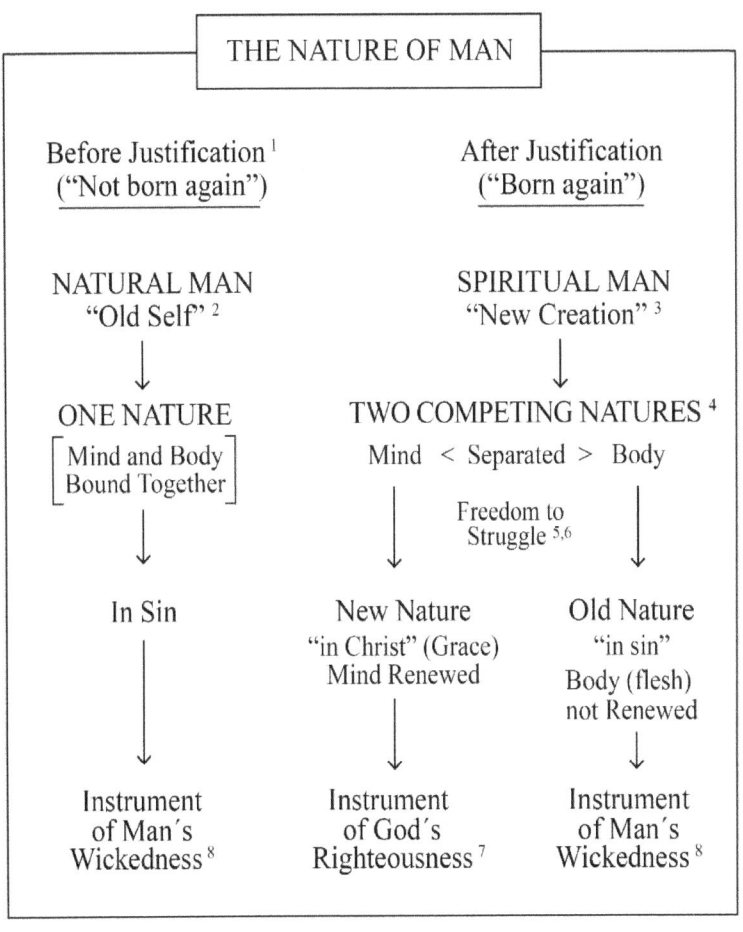

1. Romans 5:1-2; John 3:1-5
2. Romans 6:6
3. 2 Cor. 5:17
4. Romans 7:22-23, 6:13
5. R. Pope 01/17/16 Sermon
6. Galatians 5:17
7. Romans 6:13
8. Romans 6:13

How is the Spiritual Man a "new creation"?

Like an egg splits to create twins, upon being born again a man's old self[128] (i.e. mind and body bound together in sin) *separates* into two natures: the mind is renewed in Christ, but the body (flesh) is not renewed and remains in sin. The newly converted Spiritual Man has the ability, with Christ's help, to "live a new life."[129]

What does that look like?

The Spiritual Man is "no longer ruled by sin" and no longer a "slave to sin."[130] He is no longer "free from the control of righteousness."[131] Like discarding soiled garments for new clothes, the "old self" is taken off and the "new self" put on.[132] The Spiritual Man experiences a newness of life and pursues a new purpose: to be God's "instrument of righteousness," rather than man's "instrument of wickedness."[133] What does it mean to be God's "instrument of righteousness"? The Prayer of St. Francis provides guidance:

> Lord, make me an instrument of Your peace;
> Where there is hatred, let me sow love;
> Where there is injury, pardon;
> Where there is doubt, faith;
> Where there is despair, hope;
> Where there is darkness, light;
> And where there is sadness, joy.
>
> O Divine Master,
> Grant that I may not so much seek
> To be consoled, as to console;
> To be understood, as to understand;
> To be loved, as to love;
> For it is in giving that we receive,
> It is in pardoning that we are pardoned,
> And it is in dying that we are born to Eternal Life.
> Amen.

As God's instrument of righteousness, does a Spiritual Man no longer sin? No. While his renewed mind "delights in God's law" and he seeks to be an "instrument" of God's righteousness, his flesh still wanders into unrighteousness.[134] Paul summarized the struggle well in Romans 7:15: "I do not understand what I do. For what I want to do I do not do, but what I hate I do." The outcome? Pastor Randy Pope explained that the Spiritual Man has the "freedom to struggle"[135] between his two competing natures.

He lives out his two natures in a daily battle trying to be an "instrument of righteousness" (from mind renewed) rather than an "instrument of wickedness"[136] (from body not renewed). When he sins, he is forgiven through confession. However, once justification occurs (being "born again"), he cannot be outside of God's love. He cannot lose his salvation. He will lose some daily battles, but he cannot lose the war, because he has Christ's righteousness. After justification, this lifelong process of being an instrument of righteousness and pursuing God's holiness is called sanctification.

The ongoing struggle (and failure) between what we ought to do (mind renewed) versus what we actually do (body not renewed) reveals the need for grace from a savior. The Christian belief that man's nature is bad (selfish) and reliant upon a savior is not widely believed in theory or application. This small following requires only a narrow path.

I challenge you to think about it like this: The type of man we are dictates what we chase after and whether we seek a savior. To that end, what type of man are you: Moral Man, Natural Man, or Spiritual Man? Before you answer, let me throw one more wrench into the equation.

Consider this controversial statement: The Moral Man doesn't exist. There, we said it. The truth is, we're just not as good as we think we are. Not even close. "Most people strongly believe they are just, virtuous, and moral; yet regard the average person as distinctly less so."[137] Ninety-eight percent of us think we're in the nicest 50 percent of the population.[138]

We're delusional when it comes to judging our own goodness against that of everyone else. We confess this delusion every New Year's Eve. According to a Marist Poll, "being a better person" was the number-one New Year's resolution in 2018, tied with "losing weight."[139] If we claim to be so good, why do we strive to be even "better"? In truth, we crave to be "better" because deep down we know we're not that good, not selfless.

You might be saying, "Hogwash." Many of us cling to the belief that we are good, self-sufficient people (and therefore in no particular need for a savior). Take charity, for example. Say someone gives big money to build a charity hospital to serve the poor. Doesn't that prove he or she is intrinsically a good person? Not at all. The gift is only half the story; the *motive* behind the gift is the big reveal. Is his or her name on the hospital building? Is there an annual dinner thrown in his or her honor before the community elites? Was the gift trumpeted in the news? Does he or she get more satisfaction from giving resources than holding on to them?

Stay with the example of a charity hospital. If the same person *anonymously* gives big money to build a hospital to serve the poor, that proves a Moral Man exists, right? Not really. First, it is amazing how many anonymous gifts don't remain that way for long, or perhaps the benefactor prefers anonymity.

Ken Langone is an American businessman and generous philanthropist. He is one of the founders of the Home Depot. In 1999, he and his wife gave $100 million to the NYU Medical Center with the stipulation that it be *anonymous*. He then gave another $200 million anonymously. That gave the leadership at NYU Medical an idea. They requested that Langone permit the disclosure of his gifts and attach his name to the medical center thinking it would encourage other big-hitters to come forward with their own "major gifts."[140]

Langone agreed. His gifts were made public, and other benefactors did come forward with major gifts to enhance the medical center to benefit the community—a real success story for all involved. Langone discussed his anonymous gifts in his book, *I Love Capitalism*. To his credit, he acknowledges the pride his charity brings him, but explains it's less about "vanity" than helping others. The struggle is real.

Second, anonymous gifts are not selfless, regardless of whether they stay secret. A person always has a reason for why giving away his money is more important than keeping it, even if done anonymously. The old story goes that a reporter tracked down an anonymous big donor and revealed his identity to the local townspeople. The donor was not happy. When the reporter asked why the donor wanted to remain anonymous rather than enjoy the adulation of a grateful community, he replied, "Now every Tom, Dick, and Harry will be bugging me for money and I'll have no peace." There is such a thing as the anonymous selfish donor.

The highest evidence that charitable giving remains a selfish endeavor is that it rarely ever affects the lifestyle of the donor. A donor could give $100 million (as Langone did), but his lifestyle remains unchanged. The private jets and second homes remain. Don't misunderstand; we're not knocking Langone. We stand up and applaud him and all the good his gifts will do. Nor are we knocking wealth, capitalism, or charitable giving. Generous giving supports major institutions in nearly every community. But let's not deceive ourselves. Doing charitable acts that help people is laudable, but don't confuse doing good with acting selflessly. We are all very skilled in the art of making our selfishness look selfless. There is no Moral Man.

In summary, the door to our spiritual journey is locked by earthly cravings. If we believe there is nothing wrong with pursuing our cravings (or believe there is something wrong with them but can't break free of keeping up with the Joneses), then earthly pursuits will lock out any meaningful spiritual pursuits. Embracing the Spiritual Man worldview and turning away from the control of our earthly cravings is the first lock to crack open in order to make spiritual progress. But only the first lock. The locks of lies and doubts still bar the door to our spiritual formation.

• CHAPTER 7 •

THE LIES LOCK

"Frankly, my dear, I don't give a damn." This line delivered by Rhett Butler is usually mistaken as the last line of the iconic film *Gone with the Wind*. It isn't. The movie's actual last line is one of the great all-time lies when applied to Christianity.

In the final scene, Rhett is fed up and leaving Scarlett O'Hara forever. Scarlett begs him to stay. She apologizes for past mistreatment and professes her eternal love for him. Rhett is unmoved, delivers his famous line, dons his snappy hat, and disappears into the mist. Scarlett is distraught. Without him, life has no meaning. She thinks, *There must be some way to get him back.* And then Scarlett delivers the final lines: "I can't think about it now. I'll go crazy if I do! I'll think about it tomorrow. After all, tomorrow is another day."

The music crests. The credits roll.

That is what we call the Scarlett O'Hara promise: "I'll think about it tomorrow. After all, tomorrow is another day." Well, tomorrow is not guaranteed. Therefore, thinking about an existential topic tomorrow (i.e. the existence of God) is likewise not guaranteed. The Scarlett O'Hara promise is a lie.

The world keeps us very busy on external things such as family, career, relationships, and screens. Even if there is a spark of spiritual curiosity, it's too often snuffed out by the demands of everyday living. But that's okay, as we rationalize there will be time later to investigate eternal matters such as God and Church. The result? We build our lives on what is seen (external) rather than what is unseen (eternal), thinking we have plenty of time to figure out the Christianity thing later. Of the approximate 2.8 million people that die in the US each year, how many believed the lie that they had plenty of time to investigate Christianity before passing? And how many never got around to it?

Does God have a plan for our individual lives? Hmm. I'll think about that tomorrow. After all, tomorrow is another day. Is Christ's promise of eternal life for those that follow Him real? Hmm. I'll think about that tomorrow. After all, tomorrow is another day. How many tomorrows do we have left? We probably should get around to doing a spiritual investigation. Let's put it on the calendar—wait for it—tomorrow, right after we watch the end of the ball game and update our social media.

Tomorrow is not guaranteed. It never has been. Scarlett O'Hara's promise is a lie. This lie is a lock preventing our spiritual formation. To break the lie lock, we better start our spiritual investigation now. RIGHT NOW! It's time to take on the most formidable lock of all barring the door to spiritual formation: doubt.

CHAPTER 8

THE DOUBTS LOCK

The Snake Question

Bill Maher is a comedian, commentator, and long-time host of the HBO show *Real Time with Bill Maher*. He is an atheist. He often tackles religious topics, and even made a movie called *Religulous* scrutinizing the world's major religions.

When interviewing Ross Douthat, a *New York Times* columnist and Bible-believing Catholic, on his book *Bad Religion*, Maher challenged the Bible's authenticity. He posed the classic snake question, "How can an otherwise very intelligent person [referring to Douthat] believe in the talking snake?" This being a reference to the snake talking to Eve in the Garden of Eden in Genesis 3:1. But that is just scratching the surface. The snake question is only the beginning. If you really want to feel challenged, try answering these questions:

- Did God really create the world in seven days? (Genesis 1)
- Can God speak through a burning bush? (Exodus 3:1–3)
- Did Moses really part the Red Sea? (Exodus 14:21–31)
- Did Jesus really raise Lazarus from the dead? (John 11:1–44)
- Is Jesus' virgin birth possible? (Matthew 1:18–25)
- If there is a loving God, why do bad things happen to good people?
- If there is a loving God, why permit those He created to suffer eternally in hell?

- Why does God want to be glorified in all things?

How did we do in answering those questions? Skeptics are very good at cherry-picking Bible verses to create doubt and even ridicule the Bible's authority. *Falsus in uno, falsus in omnibus*—the Latin phrase meaning, "False in one thing, false in everything." Skeptics argue that if the scriptures are false in one verse, they are false in all verses, including the gospel message. Maher makes a simple point: Snakes can't talk; therefore, the Bible is not reliable and is insufficient to support the case for Christ.

Maybe Bill Maher is not our cup of tea. How about Albert Einstein? Are we interested in what his massive brain thought about the legitimacy of God? Unfortunately, more doubts. Einstein summarized his own doubts this way: "I cannot conceive of a personal God who would . . . sit in judgment on creatures of his own creation."[141] This is a curious rebuttal. Anyone with children knows that we sit in judgment of our little creations on what seems like a daily basis. Yet his point is taken—none of us seek eternal damnation for our children. If Einstein had doubts, then maybe we should all have a little humility and admit that not all religious matters lend themselves to scientific proof.

What about the other side of the doubt aisle? There are those who beat the spiritual doubts. Maybe someone like Mother Teresa, right? Nope, still more doubts. As it turns out, the "saint of the gutters," Nobel Peace Prize winner, and canonized saint had extreme doubts about God's existence in her life for nearly her entire ministry. After her death, her correspondence was edited into the book *Mother Teresa: Come Be My Light*. As reported in *Time* magazine, "The letters, many preserved against her wishes . . . reveal that for the last nearly half-century of her life she felt no presence of God whatsoever."[142] Ouch.

If Einstein, the intellectual giant, and Mother Teresa, the spiritual giant, had doubts, then where does that leave the rest of us? Actually, in exactly the same place. Everyone brings doubts to the religious equation. The best we can do is get our doubts organized so we can conduct an efficient spiritual investigation and not be distracted by the imponderables in the Bible.

42. DOUBT THE BIG QUESTIONS, NOT THE SMALLER ONES

We all have spiritual doubts. Doubt isn't a stumbling block to belief; rather, it is an essential part of the faith journey for the sincere seeker. We only have so much time to investigate the claims of Christ, so let's get our doubts organized. Otherwise, we'll be chasing our investigative tails, getting distracted, and probably giving up the spiritual search. Einstein questioned God's judgment. Mother Teresa questioned God's presence in her life. Maher questioned the veracity of the Bible. Are these proper targets for doubt?

Heck no! Why not? Because they miss the big point. The focus of our spiritual investigation is not whether a snake talked, a bush burned, or if Mary and Joseph had sex. These are mere distractions from the main event. There is one question in human history above all others that we should focus our doubt on: *Did the resurrection and ascension of Jesus Christ happen?*

If Jesus did not rise from the dead and ascend to heaven, then Christianity is fraudulent and there is no eternal life through Jesus. If the resurrection never happened, then who cares if a snake talked or a bush didn't burn up? On the other hand, if Christ rose from the dead and is the only pathway to eternal life, that is something to act on and not pass up. Therefore, life's threshold question boils down to this: Is there sufficient evidence to reasonably believe in Christ's resurrection and ascension? If we want to doubt something, doubt and investigate that! How we answer that will govern our lives — earthly and eternal.

43. WHAT IS THE ANSWER?

The world responds with a resounding "NO!" Most of the world does not buy the resurrection or that Jesus is the only way to heaven and eternal life. Ninety-two percent of all Americans agree that Jesus was a real person, but only 56 percent believe that he is divine or God incarnate.[143] Overwhelmingly, the world rejects Christ (and His resurrection work) as the *only pathway* to heaven and eternal life.[144] This is doubted by billions and billions of people. According to the Pew Research Center, as of 2015, there were an estimated 7.3 billion people in the world.[145] The top five religious groups broke down as follows:

1. Christians: 2.3 billion
2. Muslims: 1.8 billion
3. Unaffiliated: 1.2 billion
4. Hindus: 1.1 billion
5. Buddhists: 0.5 billion

The groups after Christians, by definition, reject that Christ is the only pathway to eternal life. Most Americans agree with Muslims, Hindus, and Buddhists on that point.

In America, according to the Pew Research 2014 Religious Landscape Study, "Two-thirds of those who identify with a religious group say many religions (not just their own) can lead to eternal life. This is the dominant viewpoint of mainline Protestants (80%) and Catholics (79%)."[146]

Such skepticism isn't new and existed even among Christ's followers. The apostle Thomas ("doubting Thomas") followed Jesus, saw His teachings and countless miracles, and even courageously summoned the other disciples to travel with Jesus to Judea so "that we may die with him."[147] Thomas then turned around and denied the resurrection, the essence of Christianity.[148] Explain that.

What is *our* answer to the resurrection question?

Do we agree with the world?

Nope.

We believe there is good evidence to believe in Christ's resurrection and eternal life with the father. Yet, if we really want to investigate whether Christ's resurrection and ascension happened, it's going to require homework. Bring doubt to this question and make up your own mind. To explore the validity of the resurrection, please refer to Appendix A, which has a list of suggested reading materials arguing both sides of the resurrection question.

Realistically, to have a successful investigation, going it alone is a losing proposition. Who will encourage us to persevere? Who will hold us accountable to keep going when we don't feel like it? Who will test our thinking? If we're going to sustain a spiritual investigation, let's admit we need help.

We have four suggestions to increase the odds that we will finish what we started and face our doubts.

Suggestion #1: Join a Team

Don't go at it alone. If you want to stop drinking, join Alcoholics Anonymous. If you're struggling with mental-health issues, join a support group. If you want to get fit, join a gym. The simple act of being with like-minded people dramatically increases the likelihood of completing the investigation, regardless of the outcome.

The upshot: Join a church (or at least attend a church) to consistently hear the gospel and comprehend the Christian worldview. Better yet, join a small group or Bible study to be around other Christians applying (imperfectly) Christ's teachings to their individual lives. The Lone Ranger mentality is a sure way to give up on our spiritual journeys. Even the Lone Ranger had Tonto.

Suggestion #2: Stay in the Bible

Read a little bit each day. Start with just one chapter of one book. Stay with that goal until you feel ready to increase the pace. The more we read, the more we'll be convicted to continue reading. Each reading will pierce our hearts little by little to focus on the things of God rather than the things of man; the things of the eternal rather than the things of the external.

Give it a try. Besides, it might be a nice break from scrolling through our social-media feeds.

Suggestion #3: Memorize One Scripture Verse

There is no downside here. The Bible is chock-full of life lessons, regardless of whether we believe in the resurrection. Take advantage of its wisdom. Some of this wisdom includes:

- "Children, obey your parents in the Lord, for this is right."[149] (That seems like a good one to remember and remind our children.)
- "Let us not become weary in doing good, for at the proper time we will reap a harvest if we do not give up."[150] (This universal message of not quitting isn't even particularly spiritual.)

Whatever the life topic—death, love, joy, pain, struggle, you name it—the Bible brings insight to all life's challenges and dilemmas.

Suggestion #4: Follow, then Believe (Maybe)

The final suggestion is the natural extension of the prior three. While we're in the Bible, why not take a test ride in following Jesus' teachings in our own lives? Maybe it will lead to belief. What do we have to lose?

Jesus taught us to love our neighbors.[151] He taught us to live by the Golden Rule.[152] He taught us to forgive one another.[153] Sounds pretty good, right? Wouldn't we be happier if we followed these teachings?

Something interesting may happen if we decide to apply Jesus' teachings to our lives. It may lead to *belief* in Christ's resurrection and His saving power. Follow, then believe.[154] The early apostles exemplified the "follow first and believe later" model. Andrew and Simon were the very first apostles called by Christ. Jesus said to them, "Come, follow me, and I will make you fishers of men."[155] Andrew and Simon didn't comprehend the divinity of Christ when they dropped their fishing nets. That came later. They didn't understand the resurrection. It hadn't happened. They followed first, then believed later.

The Jewish phrase for this concept is Na'aseh v'nishma. Translation: We will do and then we will understand. But following first doesn't always lead to understanding and belief.

Let's revisit the apostle Thomas. He walked with Christ. He ate with Christ. He saw Christ's miracles. Yet he not only doubted Christ's resurrection, he flat-out denied it. He came around and believed only after he put his fingers in Jesus' crucifixion wounds.[156] That experiential confirmation isn't on the table for the rest of us. Thomas would still be a doubter in today's world since Christ's physical wounds are not available for inspection.

The same is true for many of our founding fathers. They read Christ's teachings, believed in a Creator God, and still rejected Christ as the saving messiah. Thomas Jefferson, James Madison, and Benjamin Franklin rejected Jesus Christ as the only pathway to eternal life. Jefferson took scissors and literally cut the resurrection story out of his Bible.

Most of the world won't get to the belief in Christ as the savior. It is a narrow path. Doubt leads to spiritual rejection. The doubts are real and lock out many from opening the door to God. Yet if we follow and understand Christ's teachings and God puts a belief in our hearts to accept Christ through faith, then we're ready to be Christians. If no heart change happens, then we're not. Every person in human history is confronted by the same wager: to accept doubt or accept faith.

• CHAPTER 9 •

THE WAGER

44. PASCAL'S WAGER ON GOD

Blaise Pascal (1623–1662) was a French mathematician and philosopher who argued that a rational person should sincerely believe in God based on probability theory. If God exists, the believer is rewarded eternally for his faith. If God does not exist, the believer is not punished anyway. (Except for the short-term selfish debauchery missed out on by the mistaken belief in God, according to Pascal's critics.) This theory is known as Pascal's wager.

	God Exists	God Does Not Exist
Wager for God	Eternal Gain	Status Quo
Wager against God	Eternal Misery	Status Quo

45. THE WAGER THAT ALL MEN FACE

From Pascal in seventeenth-century France to us in this moment, the wager never changes; we all face it. The destiny of every man, without exception, is sealed by this single wager:

Follow man to eternal death
or
Follow Christ to eternal life

The consequence of free will brings either eternal blessing or hazard from this solemn choice. Sooner or later, the great wondering ends and eternity begins.

CHOOSE AS IF YOUR LIFE DEPENDS ON IT—
BECAUSE MAYBE IT DOES.

• CHAPTER 10 •

THE GOSPEL GAMES

In this chapter, we aim to crack open the locks (cravings, lies, and doubts) and take the "Follow Christ" side of Pascal's wager because of two foundational beliefs: (Belief #1) God has a plan for us, and (Belief #2) the gospel message accomplishes God's plan for us. God's plan is easy to understand, but the gospel message is hard to understand.

To simplify the gospel message (Belief #2), we're using two game analogies: the Rubik's cube and poker. Hence, our chapter title, "The Gospel Games." Comparing the gospel message to parlor games? Blasphemous! Okay, maybe a little. But here's the thing. The gospel message is the foundation of Christianity, essential for accomplishing God's plan for us. So why is it so hard to *understand, remember, and communicate* to others? If we asked ten people, "What is two plus two?" we'd immediately get the same answer. Simple! Ask those same ten people, "What is the gospel message?" we'd get answers all over the place, if any at all. Hard! Why can't the gospel message be simple?

In this chapter we aim ridiculously high: first, to understand God's plan for us (Belief #1), and second, to understand, remember, and communicate to others how the gospel message accomplishes God's plan for us (Belief #2). Will we hit the mark? That's wishful thinking. But maybe we'll make some progress. One thing is for sure: God's plan and the gospel message will be boiled down to one diagram and one sentence for consideration.

46. WHAT IS GOD'S PLAN FOR US?

God's plan is to rescue sinful man from eternal death. That's it in a sentence. Christianity is nothing more than a rescue operation born out of God's unfailing love for man, his creation.

God's rescue plan is revealed in the Bible for all to see. It's in John 3:16—the most famous passage of all—"For God so loved the world that he gave his one and only Son, that whoever believes in him shall not perish but have eternal life." Through Christ, God rescues us from death and provides us with eternal life. That is God's plan. But how does God accomplish it?

47. HOW GOD ACCOMPLISHES HIS RESCUE PLAN FOR US

Jesus Christ is the mission leader (code name "Savior") of God's rescue operation. His combat weapon: the gospel message. Christ and the gospel message accomplish God's rescue plan for us.

48. HOW DOES THE GOSPEL MESSAGE ACCOMPLISH GOD'S RESCUE PLAN?

Buckle up.

God's rescue plan is easy to understand, but how God accomplishes it through Christ and the gospel message is hard to understand. The gospel message is the ultimate spiritual Rubik's cube: handled by many, understood by few. Raise your hand if you ever solved the Rubik's cube. We thought not. It's a mystery, much like the gospel message. On that positive note, we march onward.

49. KILL ALL THE CONFUSING CHURCH WORDS

The first thing we do is kill all of the confusing church words.

Christianity in general and the gospel message in particular are hard to understand because there are too many words thrown around explaining them. For example, some commonly heard confusing church words include *the fall, sin, gospel, grace, good news, born again, faith, justification, righteousness, sanctification, glorification, redemption, restoration,* and *consummation*, to name just a few. And *predestination*? Let's not go there.

Got all those? Do we know what they all mean and how they connect to one another to accomplish God's rescue plan? Hardly.

The first step to comprehension is to use simple words put in a logical sequence.

Definitions please! The simpler, the better.

50. GOSPEL: ONE WORD, TWO MEANINGS

The reason the gospel message isn't easy to understand is because it has *two different meanings*—a means component and an ends component. If we don't understand the gospel's dual meaning, we won't understand and remember the overall message and how it accomplishes God's rescue plan.

Meaning #1 (Ends): Broadly speaking, the gospel message refers to the "good news" of what God has done for us through the life, resurrection, and reign of Jesus Christ.[157] Translation: gospel = good news, whatever that means.

Meaning #2 (Means): Specifically speaking, at the core of the gospel message lies the doctrine of grace. Translation: gospel = grace, whatever that means.

So does the gospel message mean "good news" or "grace," or both? And what do those words mean anyway?

51. THE BIG THREE "G" WORDS

To understand the gospel message, we must understand and connect the big three "G" words: gospel, good news, and grace. Let's start building our diagram.

God's Rescue Plan for Man (Belief #1)
↓
Gospel Message Accomplishing God's Rescue Plan (Belief #2)

Grace ⟶ Good News

52. SOLVING "GOOD NEWS" (THE "ENDS")

Meaning #1 (the "Ends")

Gospel   =   Good News

What is the Good News?

The gospel message broadly refers to the "good news" of what God has done for us through the life, resurrection, and reign of Jesus Christ. This begs two questions: (1) What is this good news, and (2) how do we get it?

The good news is simple: A sinner is transformed and saved from *eternal death*. Using a worldly analogy, a death-row inmate receives a last-minute pardon as he's walking to the electric chair. That's good news for the inmate; he's saved.

But the gospel provides a second piece of good news. The person saved from eternal death also enjoys a better life now. Let's not confuse a better life now with better life circumstances. Being a Christian doesn't mean we'll be a master-of-the-universe bigshot type jetting around in a private plane calling the shots. Not at all. Being a Christian usually means our life circumstances decline given the prevailing disapproving secular culture. But if we accept Christ—more on how that happens later—we are a changed person experiencing a *newness of life* for the rest of our earthly existence with the ability to experience peace and joy despite the cultural storms and crappy life circumstances around us.

So, to summarize, there are two pieces of good news. First, we get a *permanent future benefit.* We defeat the grave and experience eternal life, accomplishing God's rescue plan. And second, we get an *immediate, albeit temporary, benefit.* We enjoy a better life now.

Whoever came up with the term "good news" is a lousy marketer. This isn't good news, it's great news! This is the best news in human history!

Next question: How do we get such good news for our lives? That is where grace (gospel meaning #2) comes in.

53. SOLVING GRACE (THE "MEANS")

Meaning #2 (the "Means")

Gospel　　=　　Grace

The gospel message also means "grace." Have you ever watched a pastor try to explain grace to a congregation, and then try to get them to remember its meaning the following Sunday? It's not easy, hence the Rubik's cube metaphor. Since getting grace is a prerequisite to getting the gospel's good news and accomplishing God's rescue plan, we must solve grace.

What Is Grace?

Grace is the two-part saving work that Jesus Christ did on the cross for us—specifically, (part 1) Christ took our sins unto Himself and by his death paid the penalty for our sins, leaving us forgiven; and (part 2) Christ gave us His righteousness, transforming our nature from Natural Man to Spiritual Man (as discussed in Chapter 6). As Peter put it, "For Christ died for sins once for all, the righteous for the unrighteous, to bring you to God."[158] Grace transforms our hearts by ridding us of our sins and replacing it with Christ's righteousness, which is a good thing, because Romans 6:23 warns, "For the wages of sin is death." By removing sin from our hearts, grace saves us from death. Through this two-part saving mechanism, grace demonstrates God's unfailing love for man.

How to Remember Grace? Think "Switcheroo"

Grace is easy to forget. We need a memory aid for grace. Some call Christ's two-part saving work an "exchange," "trade," or "swap"—all accurate, but we introduce another term to remember the grace transaction: *switcheroo*. Yes, it's a real word. Merriam-Webster defines switcheroo as "a surprising variation: reversal." We like switcheroo because it adds a veneer of whimsy (maybe too much) and accuracy to grace's description.

Initially, and there should be no debate here, switcheroo is a fun word to say and therefore easier to remember. Who doesn't like saying "the old switcheroo"? Try it! Say, "For God so loved the world, He gave His only begotten Son, and Jesus pulled the old switcheroo to save sinful man."

Beyond whimsy, switcheroo infuses *surprise* into grace's meaning. And grace is surprising. By grace, we dispose of something bad (sin) in exchange for something good (Christ's righteousness), accomplishing God's plan of rescuing us from eternal death. Grace is a killer deal for us. And killer deals are surprising.

In summary, grace means the two-part saving work that Jesus Christ did on the cross on our behalf—he took our sins and we took His righteousness. We call this the switcheroo. To remember grace, think switcheroo.

What Isn't Grace?

It's not about us or our work.

Through the crucifixion, Christ has done it all and paid for the gift of grace, giving believers eternal life. The gift of grace is not something we earned. It is not about our good works. We did nothing. And this truth is a good thing, for as D. L. Moody famously commented, "I'm glad we are saved by grace, not by good works. Because . . . I don't wanna sit in heaven and listen to everybody brag for eternity how they got there."

Now that we have described what grace is and what it isn't, let's update our diagram.

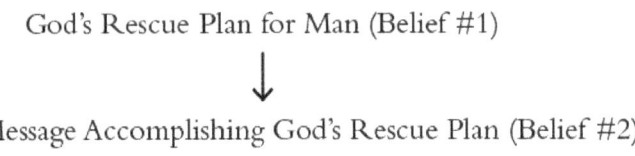

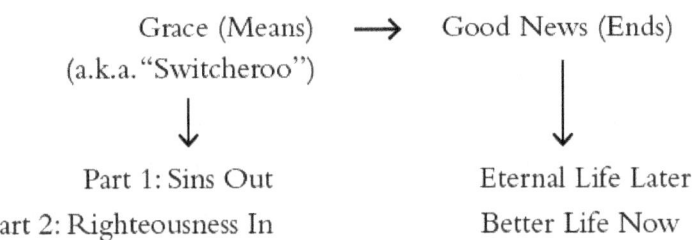

How Do We Get Grace to Accomplish Our Rescue?

The good news sounds great. And grace is how we get the gospel's good news. So far, so good. But what instructions must we follow to get the gift of grace? Well, like receiving any other gift, all one does is *accept it*. How? By faith alone. As Paul explained to the Ephesians, "For by grace you have been saved through faith. And this is not your own doing; it is the gift of God."[159]

54. ADDING THE "F" WORD TO ACCOMPLISH GRACE

We get grace by "faith alone." What does that mean?

What Is Faith?

As explained in Hebrews 11:1, "Now faith is confidence in what we hope for and assurance about what we do not see." As Ted Schroder put it, having faith "means acting without final knowledge, or proven certainty. It means we go before we know the final results."[160] Simply put, faith means taking an action based on the hope of a future outcome that we can't currently see or conclusively prove.

What Do We Put Our Faith in to Get Grace?

Not what, but whom. *We accept the gift of grace by putting our faith in Jesus Christ alone,* meaning we follow God's prompting and take decisive action to *turn* from sin and *trust* in Christ as our Lord and Savior, thereby saving ourselves and cementing our love relationship with God. We must go with Christ before we know with scientific certainty the authenticity of His claims.

Let's see if we understand. We're supposed to put our faith in a person that we've never seen (i.e. Jesus Christ) for doing something never proven (i.e. the resurrection) so we can live eternally in a supposed paradise (i.e. heaven). That sounds extremely shaky. Why would we do that?

We wouldn't, unless we had faith in the accuracy of two things we can't prove: (1) what Christ did (His saving work on the cross), and (2) what Christ promised (eternal life to His followers, accomplishing God's rescue plan).

What did Christ do? Through His resurrection, He ascended to heaven to enjoy eternal life with the Father. No one can be left wondering how it works. Christ showed us the way from physical death to eternal life. He walked the resurrection walk.

What did Christ promise? To His followers, He promised eternity in heaven with Him. In John 10:27-28, Jesus said, "My sheep listen to my voice; I know them, and they follow me. I give them eternal life, and they shall never perish; no one will snatch them out of my hand." To hammer home the promise, in John 14:6, Jesus added, "I am the way and the truth and the life. No one comes to the Father except through me." Is this promise of eternal life to Christ's followers trustworthy? We won't know for sure until we pass away from this realm.

Here's the thing. The "big reveal" moment is coming. One day—and it's coming soon—we will all pass away and instantly know whether the promised heaven is true or false. But once the big reveal happens, we won't be able to change course. The wager—faith or doubt—is fixed before the eternal outcome is known. We concede that we can't verify what Christ did or His promises to His followers by the scientific method. We further concede that we can only get grace by "faith alone," meaning by taking an action based on our hope that Christ's promise of eternal life for His followers is real. And again, the "faith alone" action is to *turn* from sin and *trust* in Christ alone as our Lord and Savior.

How to Accomplish the "Faith Alone" Action

We get grace by "faith alone." How? Prayer. Many profess their faith in Christ through a prayer, referred to as the "sinner's prayer." However, saying a prayer in and of itself is not enough if not accompanied by a changed heart and nature. If you say the sinner's prayer but continue unaffected as an "instrument of wickedness"[161] rather than God's "instrument of righteousness," then the desired faith profession has probably fallen short and not resulted in being born again. Of course, we could be wrong, as judgment belongs to God, not man.

Bottom line: All that is required to receive the gift of grace is a sincere profession of faith, meaning an affirmative decision to *turn* from sin and *trust* in Christ as your Lord and Savior and *follow* him. This is done through prayer. There are no magic scripts to follow to become a Christian. A minister may be present, but one is not required. Profess the substance to God. In other words, put your trust in Jesus Christ alone, worrying less about the form. People profess faith in Christ their own way, but it must be a sincere profession of faith in order to become a Christian.

55. GOD'S PLAN (BELIEF #1) AND THE GOSPEL MESSAGE ACCOMPLISHING GOD'S PLAN (BELIEF #2) IN ONE DIAGRAM AND ONE SENTENCE

Now that we have added faith and prayer to the mix, let's update our diagram and sentence.

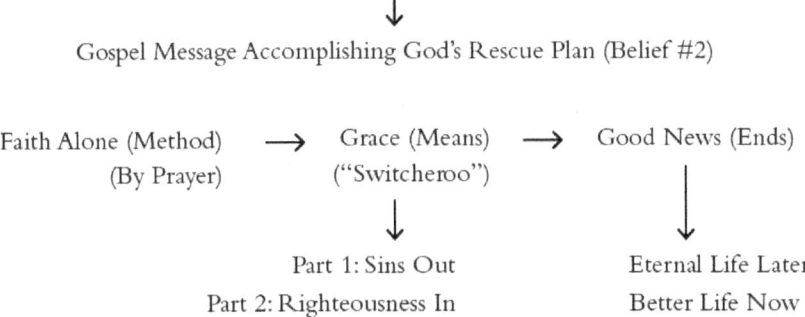

Faith in Christ begets ***grace*** ("switcheroo": our sins out/Jesus' righteousness in), which begets the ***good news*** of eternal life, accomplishing **God's rescue plan**.

Did we solve the spiritual Rubik's cube that is the gospel message? Did we make the gospel message simpler so it can be understood, remembered, and shared with others? Hard to say, but before answering, we offer a poker story in a final effort to simplify and make memorable the grace component of the gospel message.

56. GRACE ILLUSTRATED BY A POKER GAME

Gift v. Poker Metaphor

Throughout this chapter, we have referred to grace as a gift. The gift metaphor has been used by the church since the first century. In Ephesians 2:8, Paul preached the gospel to the Ephesians: "For it is by grace you have been saved, through faith—and not from yourselves, it is the *gift* of God." There it is again, the gift metaphor to illustrate grace. If the gift metaphor was good enough for Paul, it's good enough for the rest of us.

We're not quibbling with the gift metaphor. It's the all-time, go-to metaphor to illustrate grace sanctioned by Paul himself. But would a change-of-pace metaphor be so awful? Maybe someone we're trying to reach has played poker, or gambled (basketball brackets, anyone?), or done drugs, or abused alcohol, or has a criminal record, or lives an edgy lifestyle, or—wait for it—sinned (i.e. all of us).

Grace is amazing. Why not take different approaches to describe it so people remember it? Too often, the awesome meaning of grace is lost in formal church words. Let's endeavor to make grace more memorable and less forgettable.

Forgettable

If you sit in enough churches, eventually you will hear the gospel explained by the "doctrine of double imputation." This is one of the most boring phrases ever invented by academia to describe grace. It means:

Man's sin is imputed to Jesus.
Jesus' righteousness is imputed to man.

That is a 100 percent correct description of grace, but will anyone—other than theologians—remember the term "double imputation"? Hardly. A month from now, will we be able to effectively explain the gospel message to others by trotting out the doctrine of double imputation? That is why we offered the "switcheroo" term as a better memory descriptor.

That is why the gift metaphor is constantly used to explain grace. It works. Yet even the gift metaphor needs a rest. Let's give the poker metaphor a try.

Memorable

Picture yourself in a windowless, temperature-controlled, immaculate casino where it is unclear whether it's daytime or nighttime. Beautiful people are milling about. The crowd is festive. Drinks of all types are flowing. Music is pumping. The feeling that anything can happen is in the air. The house dealer steps up to the table and takes control. He perfectly prepares the game, calling out, "Five card–draw poker! No limits! Place your bets!"

You join the table.

A man in his early thirties wearing sandals and a spotless white tunic joins your table. Jesus? My goodness, Jesus has joined your table! You are playing poker with Jesus Christ of Nazareth himself. Mysteriously, no one else joins the table.

The dealer gives a sociable glance at Jesus, as if he's been here before. The body language suggests they know each other. You think, *Is Jesus a regular here? Can't be!* Jesus says nothing, tossing his ante on the table. His gold coin looks unfamiliar compared to a casino-issued chip, but the dealer says nothing. You throw in your ante. Both of you receive the standard five cards. You review your cards. *Ugh. Nothing.* Ace high—total garbage of a hand. Jesus reviews his cards looking completely serene and unsurprised, almost like he knew what was coming.

The dealer turns to Jesus. Jesus says, "I'll stand pat," taking no new cards. *What? No cards?* That never happens. No one has the perfect hand.

The dealer turns to you and asks, "Discard or stand pat?" You discard four cards, showing your ace, and receive four new cards, hoping your discard work earns you a favorable hand. Your plan pays off: You get two more aces, giving you three of a kind—a rare hand. Your poker face is fixed, but inside you're screaming, "YES!"

Your experience tells you that by standing pat, Jesus is running an amateurish bluff. No one ever stands pat. Poker players always seek to improve their outcome through skill and work. No matter what Jesus has, your plan and your work has paid off with a stout three-aces hand—statistically, a winning hand. You decide to expose Jesus' bad plan.

Not wanting to embarrass Jesus, you make a small bet, expecting Jesus to quietly fold. He doesn't. Jesus *raises* the bet. Well, you tried to be Mr. Nice Guy, but now it's time to teach Jesus a little poker etiquette. You raise the bet, and raise again. The stakes continue to build. Onlookers notice the growing stakes and begin to crowd the table, capturing the attention of the entire casino. The atmosphere is electric. Caught up in the moment, you keep raising the stakes until you're all in; your entire life savings are on the table. Everything you've worked for is on the line. Jesus calmly puts more coins on the table, matching each increase, acting like he knows what is coming.

Doesn't Jesus know that you know he's bluffing? Doesn't Jesus know that you have worked hard to earn a rare three-of-a-kind hand? Doesn't Jesus know that your plan—not His plan—is the way to victory?

The entire casino is now watching. You are sweating. Jesus is cool as a cucumber. What if Jesus isn't bluffing? What if Jesus has the perfect hand? What if by doubting Jesus, you are about to lose everything?

The bets are final. You feel an impending doom.

As Jesus moves slightly up from his seat, the house dealer gives Him a knowing smile and calls out, "Showdown!" He instructs both players to show their cards to determine the winner. The crowd is hushed, waiting for the climax. You feel sick to your stomach thinking, *You IDIOT, this is JESUS CHRIST, the guy that defeated death!*

Suddenly, Jesus raises his hand to halt the proceedings. The house dealer smiles, as if expecting it. The moment of truth is suspended in time. Your adrenaline is off the charts! Your heart feels like it is about to explode in anticipation of what happens next.

Jesus stands up and calmly moves toward you, parting the watching crowd. He smiles, puts His hand on your shoulder, and says, "I promise this—you will have great treasure if you follow my way for you. Now stand up and switch places. I will take your seat, and you mine."

What? You're frozen. Jesus gives you an affirming nod. The house dealer gives you an affirming nod. You think, *Why is the house dealer encouraging me to follow Jesus' plan? Is he in cahoots with Jesus? What is happening here?* You're mentally wrecked, a basket case of indecision. You are FREAKING OUT!

Are you about to throw away the most epic victory of your life based on your own plan (calling Jesus' losing bluff), or gain everything by receiving Jesus' grace (switching places to take His hand)? Will you stick to your plan or accept Jesus'? Will you move in Jesus' direction or your own? Everything is riding on your decision to accept or reject Jesus' invitation to follow His plan.

Jesus and the nodding house dealer, who suddenly has a paternal air about him, prod you to action. The outcome is unknown, but you have faith in the sincerity of Jesus' promise to follow His way, not your own. You find Jesus' invitation irresistible, so you stand and turn away from your own seat and put your trust in Jesus' plan. You walk over and exchange seats with Jesus. You have His cards, and He has yours. You immediately feel differently. You have confidence in your hope of a good outcome.

Having switched places, the big reveal happens; the cards are flipped over. And what did Jesus have? Of course, a royal flush, a spotless, perfect hand. Jesus takes to Himself your three aces, the losing hand. And you take Jesus' royal flush, the winning, one-in-a-million hand. Your work in building your three-aces hand was completely meaningless. Jesus did it all. He had the perfect hand. He had the victory, but gave it all to you. Losing everything was imminent, but instead, by accepting Jesus' plan, you got it all. Complete victory.

To summarize, the poker metaphor illustrates grace. Jesus pulled the old switcheroo (grace) at the card table; he got your losing hand (your sin) and you got His winning hand (His righteousness). You win the victory (eternal life), provided you accept Jesus' invitation (by faith).

Yeah, it's probably not as good as the gift metaphor to illustrate grace. But the gift metaphor has been on duty for over two thousand years and needs a day off every now and then.

What is grace? Think of the old switcheroo illustrated by a poker game.

57. ARE WE CHRISTIANS YET?

So how can we be sure that our profession of faith was sincere, providing the assurance of eternal life? How can we be sure that we received grace, providing the good news? In the end, it's a heart thing. A sincere profession of faith produces a heart change—a heart surrendered. And a heart surrendered produces a new desire to follow God's law, pursue God's will, and advance our love relationship with God.

"Not good enough, too many platitudes," says the skeptic, adding, "How will we KNOW that the 'heart thing' happened?"

The "Fruit of the Spirit" Test: A Weak Test

We often hear that proof of a changed heart is shown by a person's "fruit." A newly minted Christian exhibits "love, joy, peace, patience, kindness, goodness, faithfulness, gentleness, and self-control"—the fruit of the spirit from Galatians 5:22–23. If there is fruit, there is evidence of a changed heart.

"Still not good enough," says the skeptic. "The 'fruit of the spirit' test is incapable of being measured in real life."

He has a point. The math gets complicated. There are nine pieces of metaphorical fruit ranging from love to self-control. Do we have to exhibit all of them, all the time, to prove a changed heart? If we exhibit six "fruits" most of the time, would that be proof enough of a changed heart? What if we exhibit all of them 80 percent of the time, but none of them 20 percent of the time? Does 80 percent compliance pass the proof test? What if we exhibit all of them, all the time, but expect something in return? Does the motive behind the demonstrated "fruit" factor into the changed-heart equation? If we do the right thing for the wrong reason, do we still get credit?

There are just too many moving parts in the "fruit of the spirit" test to be useful. We need a better test for assurance that a heart change has happened.

The Reconciler Test: A Better Test

This test is more straightforward. Are we reconcilers? It's a binary test, not a nine-part test. The concept of being a reconciler has been well covered. Chapter 4 explained the horizontal reconciler. Chapter 5 explained the vertical reconciler. If we are viewed as reconcilers accomplishing love, that's good assurance that the "heart thing" has happened and we're followers of Christ. If we're viewed as dividers perpetuating foolish controversies, that's good assurance that the "heart thing" hasn't happened and we're not followers of Christ.

Reconcilers and dividers have been around since the dawn of human history. The dividers are "in" Man. The reconcilers are "in" Christ. There are vastly more dividers than reconcilers. In Titus 3:10–11, Paul warned us to stay away from dividers and their foolish controversies, saying,

> Warn a divisive person once, and then warn them a second time. After that, have nothing to do with them. You may be sure that such people are warped and sinful; they are self-condemned.

Dividers still dominate the earth. They demand to be first, not last. They demand their rights rather than surrender them to their fellow man. Dividers are everywhere, always. This shouldn't surprise anyone because dividers are Natural Men (Chapter 6) who haven't been saved by grace. They do not have Christ's righteousness in them. They have no capacity to be anything but dividers.

If we're not sure whether we are dividers or reconcilers, then statistically we're most likely the former.

On the other hand, the reconciler is a rare breed with a rare purpose. In 2 Corinthians 5:17–20, Paul instructed,

> Therefore, if anyone is in Christ, he is a new creation; the old has gone, the new has come! All this is from God, who reconciled us to himself through Christ and gave us the *ministry of reconciliation*: that God was reconciling the world to himself in Christ, not counting men's sins against them. And he has committed to us the message of reconciliation. We are therefore Christ's ambassadors, as though God were making his appeal through us. We implore you on Christ's behalf: Be reconciled to God.

What is the ministry of Christians, or as Paul put it, "the ministry of reconciliation"? What does it mean to be a reconciler with a "ministry of reconciliation"? Two things: (1) We reconcile man to man, and (2) we reconcile man to God.

Paul made it very clear: "Be reconciled to God." But to reconcile man to God, we must first be in proper relationship with our fellow man. It makes no sense to believe we can reconcile an enemy to God. We have no persuasion over our enemies. They will do the opposite of what we implore them to do. Therefore, to reconcile man to God, we must first reconcile ourselves to our fellow man.

Remember Chapters 4 and 5, where we discussed horizontal and vertical reconcilers.

And how does a reconciler accomplish his two-part ministry of reconciling man to man (horizontal reconciliation) and then man to God (vertical reconciliation)? Through, you guessed it, love, joy, peace, patience, kindness, goodness, faithfulness, gentleness, and self-control. By using the fruit of the spirit's nine tools, the reconciler does his reconciliation work. The person that makes most situations better, not worse. The person who eases trouble and provides healing. Look for the reconciler, rather than his fruit-of-the-spirit tools, to see a person with a changed heart—a Christian.

Reconciler (Test of a Christian)

Fruit of the Spirit (Tools of Reconciler)

Love, Joy, Peace, Patience, Kindness, Goodness,
Faithfulness, Gentleness, Self-Control

In summary, are we consistently reconcilers or dividers? Harder yet, do we reconcile man to God? If yes, that is good evidence that we have a changed heart, bringing assurance that we have accepted the free gift of grace, are a child of God,[162] and have the peace of eternal life. If yes, that is good evidence that we have broken the locks barring a spiritual life (cravings, lies, and doubts) and opened the door to a Jesus-centered life.

Welcome in!
Praise God!

CLOSING AND VERDICT: DECISION TIME

58. THE CONCLUSION IS A VERDICT: ACCEPT OR REJECT THE FOREVER FATHER

All dads must decide, one way or another, whether we will go it alone or accept the Forever Father and pass the inheritance of the Almighty God to our descendants, whether our lives remain the same or new lives begin. The Life Verdict Form is ready to be completed.

LIFE VERDICT FORM

In the matter of _____
(your name) and _____
(child's name), I hereby select the following patriarch to follow and govern my life and the life of my descendants.

Please check only one line below. If you need more time to decide, check Line 1, as that is the default verdict.

    Line 1   _____ Disappearing Dad (Man)

or

    Line 2   _____ Forever Father (God)

This _____ day of _____, 20_____

Signed _____

INVITATION

If you selected Line 2 to follow the Forever Father, you have broken the locks (cravings, lies, and doubts) and opened the door to a Jesus-centered, spiritual life. On this side of the door, we enjoy the gospel's good news: a better life now and an eternal life later. Welcome!

59. NOW WHAT? ACCEPT THE INVITATION OF THE LOCAL CHURCH

Caution: This next moment is critical. Do not suffer the tragedy of stopping short. The best way to avoid a spiritual life is to stay in the world (nonbelievers) and away from the local church (believers and nonbelievers). Therefore, the logical next step is to join a local church that will connect you with a community of believers. No local church is perfect, but good ones providing community do exist. Don't stop short. Don't throw away the gospel's eternal good news for the world's temporary, unsatisfying news. Join the local church and be a messenger for the eternal. Join Christ's church in spreading the good news of the gospel message.

ACKNOWLEDGMENTS

Thank you to my youth experts: Meggie Cruser, a University of North Carolina (Chapel Hill) junior, and Virginia Cruser, a high school junior at the time of their contributions. Both have since graduated from college and launched into adulthood.

APPENDIX A

ADDITIONAL READING MATERIALS

We recommend the following resources to investigate the *evidence* regarding the validity of the resurrection and ascension. Bring skepticism to this question and make up your own mind.

Resources Supporting Jesus' Resurrection

Douthat, Ross. Believe: *Why Everyone Should Be Religious.* Zondervan, 2025.

Evans, Craig A. *Jesus and the Remains of His Day: Studies in Jesus and the Evidence of Material Culture.* Peabody, MA: Hendrickson, 2015.

Greyson, Bruce. *After: a doctor explores what near-death experiences reveal about life and beyond.* St. Martin's Essentials, 2021.

Habermas, Gary R., and Michael R. Licona. *The Case for the Resurrection of Jesus.* Grand Rapids, MI: Kregel, 2004.

Strobel, Lee. *The Case for the Resurrection.* Grand Rapids, MI: Zondervan, 1998.

Resources Disputing Jesus' Resurrection

Dawkins, Richard. *The God Delusion.* Boston/NY: Houghton Mifflin, 2006.

Komarnitsky, Kris. *Doubting Jesus' Resurrection: What Happened in the Black Box?* Stone Arrow Books, 2014.

ENDNOTES

1. Dubner, Stephen. "Interview of Daniel Kahneman: How to Launch a Behavior-Change Revolution." *Freakonomics*. Radio, October 25, 2017. http://freakonomics.com/podcast/launch-behavior-change-revolution/.
2. Drysdale, Jennifer. "Inside Brad Pitt's Relationship with Son Maddox." *Entertainment Tonight*. September 23, 2016. https://www.etonline.com/news/198869_inside_brad_pitt_relationship_with_son_Maddox.
3. Smith, Matthew. "World's Most Admired 2018." *YouGov*. April 11, 2018. https://yougov.co.uk/news/2018/04/11/worlds-most-admired-2018/.
4. "Health, United States, 2016: With Chartbook on Long-Term Trends in Health." National Center for Health Statistics. 2017. https://www.cdc.gov/nchs/data/hus/hus16.pdf#015.
5. Jones, Jeffrey M. "Majority in U.S. Do Not Have a Will." *Gallup*. May 18, 2016. http://news.gallup.com/poll/191651/majority-not.aspx.
6. Every Woman Every Child and Partnership for Maternal, Newborn & Child Health. "Progress in Partnership: 2017 Progress Report on the Every Woman Every Child Global Strategy for Women's, Children's and Adolescents' Health." Geneva: World Health Organization. 2017.
7. Miniño, Arialdi M. "Mortality Among Teenagers Aged 12–19 Years: United States, 1999–2006." Centers for Disease Control and Prevention. May 5, 2010. https://www.cdc.gov/nchs/products/databriefs/db37.htm.
8. Miniño. "Mortality Among Teenagers Aged 12–19 Years: United States, 1999–2006."
9. Miniño. "Mortality Among Teenagers Aged 12–19 Years: United States, 1999–2006."
10. Miniño. "Mortality Among Teenagers Aged 12–19 Years: United States, 1999–2006."
11. Hamilton. "National Vital Statistics Reports."
12. "Box Office History for Fast and Furious Movies." *The Numbers*. https://www.the-numbers.com/movies/franchise/Fast-and-the-Furious#tab=summary.

13. Associated Press. "Paul Walker's Estate Estimated at $25 Million." *The San Diego Union-Tribune.* September 5, 2016. http://www.sandiegouniontribune.com/sdut-paul-walkers-estate-estimated-at-25-million-2014feb04-story.html.
14. Ryan, Frank. Twitter post. August 16, 2010, 3:45 p.m. https://twitter.com/drfrankryan/status/21351373998.
15. Ryan, Frank. Twitter post. August 16, 2010, 4:10 p.m. https://twitter.com/drfrankryan/status/21353019927.
16. "Motor Vehicle Safety." Centers for Disease Control and Prevention. October 16, 2017. https://www.cdc.gov/motorvehiclesafety/teen_drivers/teendrivers_factsheet.html.
17. "Motor Vehicle Safety." Centers for Disease Control and Prevention.
18. "Distracted Driving 2015." National Center for Statistics and Analysis. March 2017. https://www.nhtsa.gov/sites/nhtsa.dot.gov/files/documents/812_381_distracteddriving2015.pdf.
19. "Teens Texting and Driving: Facts and Statistics." *TeenSafe.* January 8, 2018. https://www.teensafe.com/blog/teens-texting-and-driving-facts-and-statistics/.
20. Gonzales, Jason. "Siri Saves Teen after Truck Collapses on Him." *USA Today.* August 14, 2015. https://www.usatoday.com/story/tech/2015/08/14/siri-teen-truck-collapse/31746425/.
21. Miniño. "Mortality Among Teenagers Aged 12–19 Years: United States, 1999–2006."
22. Greenburg, Zack O'Malley. "Tupac Shakur Earning Like He's Still Alive." *Forbes.* March 2, 2012. https://www.forbes.com/sites/zackomalleygreenburg/2011/05/31/tupac-shakur-earning-like-hes-still-alive/#231c83af641e.
23. "Tupac Shakur Biography." *Biography.* January 19, 2018. https://www.biography.com/people/tupac-shakur-206528.
24. Reed, Ryan. "Tupac's Final Words Revealed by Police Officer on Scene of Murder." *CNN.* May 23, 2014. https://www.cnn.com/2014/05/23/showbiz/celebrity-news-gossip/tupac-last-words-rs/index.html.
25. VladTV. "Compton Gang Unit: Keefe D's 2Pac Murder Confession is Accurate." YouTube video, 8:44. Posted July 6, 2017.
26. "Homicide Rates Among Persons Aged 10–24 Years – United States, 1981–2010." Centers for Disease Control and Prevention. July 12, 2013. https://www.cdc.gov/mmwr/preview/mmwrhtml/mm6227a1.htm.
27. "Gangs—FBI." Federal Bureau of Investigation. May 3, 2016. https://www.fbi.gov/investigate/violent-crime/gangs.
28. "Chicago Shootings and Killings Fell in 2017." *The Washington Post.* https://www.washingtonpost.com/national/chicago-homicides-down-

in-2017-but-total-still-above/2018/01/01/d9fad2c2-def0-11e7-bbd0-9dfb2e37492a_story.html?utm_term=.e8642789ed31.
29. Rhodan, Maya. "Gun Deaths in America: CDC Data Shows Another Rise in 2016." *Time.* November 6, 2017. http://time.com/5011599/gun-deaths-rate-america-cdc-data/.
30. Boren, Cindy. "Remembering Len Bias 30 Years after His Death: 'He Was It.'" *The Washington Post.* June 19, 2016. https://www.washingtonpost.com/news/early-lead/wp/2016/06/19/remembering-len-bias-30-years-after-his-death-he-was-it/?utm_term=.368eea9eb0d9.
31. Weinred, Michael. "The Day Innocence Died." *ESPN.* http://www.espn.com/espn/eticket/story?page=bias.
32. The White House. "Eric Bolling." YouTube video, 3:09. Posted March 1, 2018. https://www.youtube.com/watch?v=LYcQ6mF1dZc.
33. Bien, Louis. "A Complete Timeline of the Ray Rice Assault Case." *SBNation.* May 23, 2014. https://www.sbnation.com/nfl/2014/5/23/5744964/ray-rice-arrest-assault-statement-apology-ravens.
34. Van Natta Jr., Don. "Transcript Shows Inconsistencies in Goodell's Testimony on Rice Matter." ESPN. December 11, 2014. http://www.espn.com/espn/otl/story/_/id/12009808/nfl-commissioner-roger-goodell-testimony-ray-rice-hearing.
35. "National Statistics on Domestic Violence." National Coalition Against Domestic Violence. https://ncadv.org/statistics.
36. Domonoske, Camila. "CDC: Half of All Female Homicide Victims are Killed by Intimate Partners." *NPR.* July 21, 2017. https://www.npr.org/sections/thetwo-way/2017/07/21/538518569/cdc-half-of-all-female-murder-victims-are-killed-by-intimate-partners.
37. Petrosky, Emiko, MD, Janet M. Blair, PhD, Carter J. Betz, MS, Katherine A. Fowler, PhD, Shane P. D. Jack, PhD, and Bridget H. Lyons, MPH. "Racial and Ethnic Differences in Homicides of Adult Women and the Role of Intimate Partner Violence—United States, 2003–2014." Centers for Disease Control and Prevention. July 18, 2017. https://www.cdc.gov/mmwr/volumes/66/wr/mm6628a1.htm.
38. Petrosky et al. "Racial and Ethnic Differences in Homicides of Adult Women and the Role of Intimate Partner Violence—United States, 2003–2014."
39. Harrop, Froma. "The Suicide Epidemic: Social, Economic, or Both?" *RealClearPolitics.* July 18, 2017. https://www.realclearpolitics.com/articles/2017/07/18/the_suicide_epidemic_social_economic_or_both_134488.html.

40. Curtin, Sally C., MA, Margaret Warner, PhD, and Holly Hedegaard, MD. "Increase in Suicide in the United States, 1999–2014." Centers for Disease Control and Prevention. April 22, 2016. https://www.cdc.gov/nchs/products/databriefs/db241.htm.
41. Curtin et al. "Increase in Suicide in the United States, 1999–2014."
42. Miniño. "Mortality Among Teenagers Aged 12–19 Years: United States, 1999–2006."
43. "Pancreatic Cancer." Centers for Disease Control and Prevention. October 26, 2016. https://ephtracking.cdc.gov/showPancreatic Cancer. action.
44. Tauber, Michelle. "His Battle Gets Tougher." *People.* January 26, 2009. https://people.com/archive/cover-story-his-battle-gets-tougher-vol-71-no-3/.
45. Tauber. "His Battle Gets Tougher."
46. "Smoking and Tobacco Use." Centers for Disease Control and Prevention. February 20, 2018. https://www.cdc.gov/tobacco/data_statistics/fact_sheets/fast_facts/index.htm.
47. "CDC: One in Four Teens Are Vaping." American Heart Association. June 10, 2016. https://news.heart.org/cdc-one-in-four-teens-are-vaping/.
48. Rockwell, Donna. "Amy Winehouse, the Reluctant Celebrity: A Parable on the Fatal Cost of Fame." *The Huffington Post.* July 13, 2016. https://www.huffingtonpost.com/donna-rockwell-psyd/amy-winehouse-the-reluctant-celebrity-a-parable-on-the-fatal-cost-of-fame_b_7782018.html.
49. Rockwell. "Amy Winehouse, the Reluctant Celebrity: A Parable On the Fatal Cost of Fame."
50. Rockwell. "Amy Winehouse, the Reluctant Celebrity: A Parable On the Fatal Cost of Fame."
51. Stern, Marlow. "Bristol Palin's Memoir: The Juiciest Excerpts." *The Daily Beast.* June 21, 2011. https://www.thedailybeast.com/bristol-palins-memoir-the-juiciest-excerpts.
52. Orloff, Brian. "Levi Johnston Claims Bristol Palin Got Pregnant Because Her Mom Was Expecting." *People.* September 14, 2011. https://people.com/celebrity/levi-johnston-claims-bristol-palin-got-pregnant-because-her-mom-was-expecting/.
53. Orloff. "Levi Johnston Claims Bristol Palin Got Pregnant Because Her Mom Was Expecting."
54. Rogers, Katie. "Bristol Palin Nets $262,500 as Abstinence Speaker: Is She Right for the Job?" *The Washington Post.* April 6, 2011. https://www.washingtonpost.com/blogs/blogpost/post/bristol-palin-nets-262500-as-abstinence-speaker-is-she-right-for-the-job/2011/04/06/AFN73rpC_blog.html?utm_ term=.6508e2eeb599.

55. Willis, Jackie. "Bristol Palin's 2009 Abstinence Pledge: 'It's a Realistic Goal for Myself.'" *Entertainment Tonight.* June 26, 2015. https://www.etonline.com/news/166908_bristol_palin_made_an_abstinence_vow_2009.
56. Sawhill, Isabel V. "Teen Pregnancy Prevention: Welfare Reform's Missing Component." *Brookings.* July 28, 2016. https://www.brookings.edu/research/teen-pregnancy-prevention-welfare-reforms-missing-component/.
57. National Campaign to Prevent Teen Pregnancy. "Whatever Happened to Childhood? The Problem of Teen Pregnancy in the United States." *Popline.* May 1997. https://www.popline.org/node/522357.
58. National Campaign to Prevent Teen Pregnancy. "Whatever Happened to Childhood? The Problem of Teen Pregnancy in the United States."
59. National Campaign to Prevent Teen Pregnancy. "Whatever Happened to Childhood?" The Problem of Teen Pregnancy in the United States."
60. Quinn, Dave. "Bobby Brown Reveals the First Time He Saw Whitney Houston Take Cocaine Was on Their Wedding Day." *People.* June 7, 2016. https://people.com/celebrity/bobby-brown-first-saw-whitney-houston-doing-coke-on-their-wedding-day/.
61. Samuels, Allison. "Whitney Houston's Private Hell and Inevitable Death." *Newsweek.* April 30, 2012. http://www.newsweek.com/whitney-houstons-private-hell-and-inevitable-death-64115.
62. "Whitney Houston Tells Diane Sawyer: 'Crack Is Whack.'" *ABC News.* December 4, 2002. https://abcnews.go.com/Entertainment/whitney-houston-tells-diane-sawyer-crack-whack/story?id=131898.
63. Lee, Chris. "Inside Whitney Houston's Violent Marriage to Bobby Brown." *The Daily Beast.* February 2, 2012. https://www.thedailybeast.com/inside-whitney-houstons-violent-marriage-to-bobby-brown.
64. Parry, Ryan. "EXCLUSIVE: 'I Saw Whitney and Bobby Brown Smoke Crack in Front of Their Five-Year-Old Daughter.' Houston's Driver Reveals the Drug Horror Childhood of Bobbi Kristina as Her Family Prepare to Say Goodbye." *Daily Mail.* February 5, 2015. http://www.dailymail.co.uk/news/article-2941425/I-saw-Whitney-Bobby-smoke-crack-daughter-just-five-Houston-s-driver-reveals-drug-horror-childhood-Bobbi-Kristina-family-prepare-say-goodbye.html.
65. D'Zurilla, Christie. "Bobby Brown at Whitney's Funeral: What Went on inside the Church?" *Los Angeles Times.* February 20, 2012. http://latimesblogs.latimes.com/gossip/2012/02/bobby-brown-whitney-houston-funeral-1.html.

66. Merriman, Rebecca. "How Bobbi Kristina Brown's Life Spiraled out of Control after Whitney's Death." *Mirror.* March 4, 2016. https://www.mirror.co.uk/3am/celebrity-news/how-bobbi-kristina-browns-life-7494274.
67. Schnurr, Samantha. "Bobbi Kristina Brown's Cause of Death Is Revealed." *E! Online.* March 4, 2016. https://www.eonline.com/news/745983/bobbi-kristina-brown-s-cause-of-death-is-revealed.
68. D'Zurilla, Christie. "Bobbi Kristina Brown's Partner, Nick Gordon, Order to Pay $36 Million in Wrongful Death Lawsuit." *Los Angeles Times.* November 17, 2016. http://www.latimes.com/entertainment/gossip/la-et-mg-nick-gordon-bobbi-kristina-brown-20161117-story.html.
69. Bryant, Tom. "Still Having the Time of My Life 25 Years On: *Dirty Dancing* Star Jennifer Grey on Patrick Swayze, Dancing, and Her 'Nose Job from Hell.'" *Mirror.* August 23, 2012. https://www.mirror.co.uk/3am/celebrity-news/jennifer-grey-on-patrick-swayze-dirty-1274628.
70. "Dove Self-Esteem Project." Dove. https://www.dove.com/us/en/stories/about-dove/dove-self-esteem-project.html.
71. "Plastic Surgery for Teenagers." American Society of Plastic Surgeons. https://www.plasticsurgery.org/news/briefing-papers/briefing-paper-plastic-surgery-for-teenagers.
72. Forster, Katie. "Britain's Unregulated Plastic Surgery Industry 'Targeting Children and Causing Mental Health Problems.'" *The Independent.* June 21, 2017. https://www.independent.co.uk/news/health/cosmetic-procedures-plastic-surgery-targeting-children-cause-for-concern-nuffield-council-of-a7801471.html.
73. Martel, Frances. "CNN First to Track Down Rep. Anthony Weiner for TV Comment on Twitter Scandal." *Mediaite.* May 30, 2011. https://www.mediaite.com/tv/cnn-first-to-track-down-rep-anthony-weiner-for-tv-comment-on-twitter-scandal/.
74. Miga, Andrew. "Rep. Weiner Says He Didn't Send Twitter Photo." NBC News. June 2, 2011. http://www.nbcnews.com/id/43236648/ns/politics-more_politics/t/rep-weiner-says-he-didnt-send-twitter-photo/#.Wwgd4EgvyUl.
75. Provenz, Jessica. "I Was Anthony Weiner's Longest-Serving Campaign Staffer. This Is What His Mayoral Run Was Really Like." *New York Magazine.* May 24, 2016. http://nymag.com/daily/intelligencer/2016/05/i-was-weiners-longest-serving-campaign-staffer.html.
76. "Study Exposes Secret World of Porn Addiction." The University of Sydney. May 10, 2012. http://sydney.edu.au/news/84.html?newsstoryid=9176.

77. Dedmon, J. "Is the Internet Bad for Your Marriage? Online Affairs, Pornographic Sites Playing Greater Role in Divorces." American Academy of Matrimonial Lawyers. Press release, 14.
78. "How Young People Use the Internet for Health Information." The Henry J. Kaiser Family Foundation. November 30, 2001. https://www.kff.org/health-costs/report/generation-rx-com-how-young-people-use/.
79. "The Digital Divide: How the Online Behavior of Teens Is Getting Past Parents." *McAfee*. June 2012. https://www.scribd.com/document/98269655/The-Digital-Divide-How-the-Online-Behavior-of-Teens-is-Getting-Past-Parents.
80. Dedmon. "Is the Internet Bad for Your Marriage?"
81. "2014 Pornography Survey and Statistics." *Proven Men Ministries*. www.provenmen.org/2014pornsurvey/.
82. "Pornography Statistics: 2015 Report." *Covenant Eyes*. http://www.covenanteyes.com/pornstats/.
83. "Pornography Statistics: 2015 Report." *Covenant Eyes*. http://www.covenanteyes.com/pornstats/.
84. "Anthony Weiner Biography." *Biography*. January 11, 2018. https://www.biography.com/people/anthony-weiner-20993229.
85. Laumann, Anne E., and Amy J. Derick. "Tattoos and Body Piercings in the United States: A National Data Set." *Journal of the American Academy of Dermatology*, 413–421. September 2006. https://www.ncbi.nlm.nih.gov/pubmed/16908345.
86. Laumann and Derick. "Tattoos and Body Piercings in the United States: A National Data Set."
87. Laumann and Derick. "Tattoos and Body Piercings in the United States: A National Data Set."
88. Laumann and Derick. "Tattoos and Body Piercings in the United States: A National Data Set."
89. "In His Own Words: George Clooney on Love, Marriage, and Amal Alamuddin." *People*. September 28, 2014. https://people.com/celebrity/george-clooney-on-amal-alamuddin-love-and-marriage/.
90. "George Clooney Talks 'Terrifying' Fatherhood and President Trump." USA Today. August 29, 2017. https://www.usatoday.com/story/life/people/2017/08/29/george-clooney-on-suburbicon-fatherhood-and-trump/105073304/.

91. Donnelly, Gabrielle. "'I'd Given Up on Being a Dad . . . but Now I've Got Twins and They Make Me Cry Four Times a Day,' Says an Exhausted (and VERY Honest) George Clooney." *Daily Mail.* September 15, 2017. http://www.dailymail.co.uk/tvshowbiz/article-4885910/George-Clooney-opens-fatherhood.html.
92. Parker, Kim, and Wendy Wang. "Modern Parenthood: Roles of Moms and Dads Converge as They Balance Work and Family." Pew Research Center's Social & Demographic Trends Project. March 14, 2013. http://www.pewsocialtrends.org/2013/03/14/modern-parenthood-roles-of-moms-and-dads-converge-as-they-balance-work-and-family/.
93. Maxwell, John (2007). *Maxwell Daily Reader.* Nashville, TN: Thomas Nelson
94. Maxwell. *Maxwell Daily Reader.*
95. Gladwell, Malcolm. *Outliers: The Story of Success.* New York: Back Bay Books, 2011. 39–40.
96. Wallace, Jennifer. "The Right Way for Parents to Question Their Teenagers." *The Wall Street Journal.* November 24–25, 2018.
97. Carnegie, Dale. *How to Win Friends and Influence People.* New York: Simon and Schuster, Inc. 50th Edition, 36.
98. Carnegie. *How to Win Friends and Influence People.* 27.
99. Pope Francis. *The Name of God Is Mercy.* New York: Random House, 2016. xix.
100. Crabtree, Sam. *Practicing Affirmation.* Wheaton, IL: Crossway. 47, 72.
101. Crabtree. *Practicing Affirmation.* 72.
102. Maloney, Jennifer. "PepsiCo CEO Indra Nooyi to Step Aside: Veteran Set to Take Helm." *The Wall Street Journal.* August 6, 2018. https://www.wsj.com/articles/pepsico-ceo-indra-nooyi-to-step-aside-1533553261.
103. Wattles, Jackie. "Pepsi CEO Indra Nooyi Gets Big Pay Bump." *CNNMoney.* March 18, 2017. https://money.cnn.com/2017/03/18/news/companies/pepsi-indra-nooyi/index.html.
104. Fortune Editors. "These Are the Top 10 Most Powerful Women in Business." *Forbes* magazine. September 21, 2017. http://fortune.com/ 2017/09/21/top-10-most-powerful-women-in-business/.
105. Singh, Yoshita. "Women Cannot Have It All: PepsiCo CEO Indra Nooyi." *Outlook India* magazine, July 3, 2014. https://www.outlookindia.com/ newswire/story/women-cannot-have-it-all-pepsico-ceo-indra-nooyi/847865.
106. Nilekani, Nandan. "Personal Side of Indra Nooyi." *Economic Times.* February 7, 2007. https://economictimes.indiatimes.com/industry/cons-products/ food/personal-side-of-indra-nooyi/articleshow/157611 5.cms.

107. Unger, Harlow Giles. *The Last Founding Father*. Cambridge, MA: Da Capro Press, 2009. 89.
108. Kralik, John. *A Simple Act of Gratitude*. New York: Hyperion, 2010.
109. Reeves, Richard V., Edward Rodrigue, and Alex Gold. "Following the Success Sequence? Success Is More Likely If You're White." *Brookings*. August 6, 2015. https://www.brookings.edu/research/ following-the-success-sequence-success-is-more-likely-if-youre-white/.
110. Wilcox, W. Bradford, and Wendy Wang. "The Millennial Success Sequence: Marriage, Kids, and the 'Success Sequence' among Young Adults." *AEI*. June 14, 2017. http://www.aei.org/publication/millennials-and-the-success-sequence-how-do-education-work-and-marriage-affect-poverty-and-financial-success-among-millennials/.
111. Wang, Wendy. "'The Sequence' Is the Secret to Success." *The Wall Street Journal*. March 27, 2018. https://www.wsj.com/ articles/the-sequence-is-the-secret-to-success-1522189894.
112. Reeves. "Following the Success Sequence? Success Is More Likely If You're White."
113. Office of Adolescent Health. "Trends in Teen Pregnancy and Childbearing." US Department of Health & Human Services. Last reviewed May 30, 2019. https://www.hhs.gov/ash/oah/adolescent-development/reproductive-health-and-teen-pregnancy/teen-pregnancy-and-childbearing/trends/index.html.
114. Rosen, Christine. "Teens Who Say No to Social Media." *The Wall Street Journal*. August 25, 2016. https://www.wsj.com/articles/teens -who-say-no-to-social-media-1472136877.
115. Goicochea, Hernan. "Battle of the Social Media Platforms: Instagram vs Snapchat." *The Bolognesi Post*. August 4, 2016. https://thebolognesipost. wordpress.com/2016/08/04/battle-of-the-social-media-platforms-instagram-vs-snapchat/.
116. Koh. "Snapchat's Teen Fans Wince as App Catches On with Their Folks." *The Wall Street Journal*. July 4, 2016.
117. Koh. "Snapchat's Teen Fans Wince as App Catches On with Their Folks."
118. Koh. "Snapchat's Teen Fans Wince as App Catches On with Their Folks."
119. Edwards, Jim. "Mark Zuckerberg Admits: 'Coolness Is Done For Us.'" *Business Insider*. September 18, 2013. http://www.businessinsider.com/mark-zuckerberg-admits-coolness-is-done-for-us-2013-9.
120. "The Prodigal Heir." Onward | Charles Schwab. Fall 2018.

121. "Teen Sex Down, New Study Shows." Centers for Disease Control and Prevention. May 1997. https://www.cdc.gov/media/pressrel/teensex.htm.
122. Frank, Robert. "Jeff Bezos Is Now the Richest of All Time—Sort of." *CNBC.* January 9, 2018. https://www.cnbc.com/2018/01/09/jeff-bezos-is-now-the-richest-of-all-time--sort-of.html.
123. Allrich, Ted. "How Much Money Is Enough?" Nasdaq.com. August 27, 2010. https://www.nasdaq.com/article/how-much-money-is-enough-cm34225.
124. Based on free material from GAPMINDER.ORG, CC-BY LICENSE
125. FREE TO USE! CC-BY GAMPINDER.ORG
126. Noonan, Peggy. "Kids, Don't Become Success Robots." *The Wall Street Journal.* March 16–17, 2019.
127. 2 Corinthians 5:17.
128. Romans 6:6.
129. Romans 6:4.
130. Romans 6:6.
131. Romans 6:20.
132. Colossians 3:9–11.
133. Romans 6:13.
134. Romans 7:22–23; Romans 6:13.
135. R. Pope. Sermon (Perimeter Church, January 17, 2016).
136. Romans 6:13.
137. Tappin, Ben, and Ryan McKay. "The Illusion of Moral Superiority." *Journal of Social Psychological and Personality Science* 8, no. 6 (October 2016).
138. Hosie, Rachel. "People Think They're Nicer Than They Actually Are, Study Finds." *Independent.* March 13, 2017. https://www.independent.co.uk/life-style/people-think-nicer-reality-self-image-see-yourself-goldsmiths-university-monarch-a7627161.html.
139. Marist Poll. "12/20: Being a Better Person & Weight Loss Top 2018 New Year's Resolutions." Marist Institute for Public Opinion. December 20, 2017. http://maristpoll.marist.edu/1220-being-a-better-person-weight-loss-top-2018-new-years-resolutions/#sthash.xg5PbWmH.dpbs.
140. Langone, Ken. *I Love Capitalism! An American Story.* New York: Portfolio, 2018.
141. Isaacson, W. *American Sketches.* New York: Simon & Schuster, 2009.
142. Van Biema, David. "Mother Teresa's Crisis of Faith." *TIME.* August 23, 2007. http://time.com/4126238/mother-teresas-crisis-of-faith/.
143. "What Do Americans Believe about Jesus? 5 Popular Beliefs." Barna Group. April 1, 2015. https://www.barna.com/research/what-do-americans-believe-about-jesus-5-popular-beliefs/.
144. John 3:36; 14:6.

145. Hackett, Conrad, and David McClendon. "Christians Remain World's Largest Religious Group, but They Are Declining in Europe." Pew Research Center. April 5, 2017. http://www.pewresearch.org/fact-tank/2017/04/05/christians-remain-worlds-largest-religious-group-but-they-are-declining-in-europe/.
146. "Chapter 1: Importance of Religion and Religious Beliefs." In "U.S. Public Becoming Less Religious," 62–63. Pew Research Center. November 3, 2015. http://www.pewforum.org/2015/11/03/chapter-1-importance-of-religion-and-religious-beliefs/#paths-to-eternal-life.
147. John 11:16.
148. John 20:24–25.
149. Ephesians 6:1.
150. Galatians 6:9.
151. Matthew 22:36–40.
152. Luke 6:31.
153. Matthew 18:21–22.
154. A. Stanley. Sermon (North Point Community Church, July 29, 2018).
155. Matthew 4:18–19.
156. John 20:26–27.
157. B. Cargo. Sermon (Perimeter Church, September 4, 2016).
158. 1 Peter 3:18.
159. Ephesians 2:8.
160. Schroder, Ted. *Buried Treasure*, Florida: Amelia Island Publishing, 2005.
161. Romans 6:13.
162. Romans 8:16.

ABOUT THE AUTHOR

J. Robb Cruser and his wife are the parents of five children and live on St. Simons Island, Georgia. He is a graduate of the College of William & Mary in Williamsburg, Virginia, and Emory University School of Law.

www.ingramcontent.com/pod-product-compliance
Lightning Source LLC
Chambersburg PA
CBHW070132080526
44586CB00015B/1665